"In a day and age when many parents, even (ill-equipped to parent their children facing a Murray to give us a powerful parental tool in anxiety and depression. With this book (and parents no longer have to be or feel ill-prep. issues. I just wish I had this book years ago.

Ed Stetzer, Executive Director, Billy Graham Center for Evangelism, Wheaton College

"Parenting is good for our prayer lives, we find, especially when sons and daughters are navigating the many anxieties that seem to coincide with the teenage years. David Murray has the practical experience and spiritual wisdom to help. Based in biblical truth and at the same time sensitive to the psychological and physiological complexities of human emotions, Murray's companion guides tell real-life stories that empower teens and their parents to understand their feelings, care well for one another, and take concrete steps toward healing together."

Phil and Lisa Ryken, President, Wheaton College, and his wife, Lisa

"In this book, David Murray comes alongside parents who may be willfully naive about or find themselves completely overwhelmed by how to help their child deal with depression, offering understandable explanations of the issues and equipping them for important conversations."

Nancy Guthrie, Bible teacher; author, *Even Better than Eden*

"Parents are the most influential and important individuals in their teenager's life. But often parents struggle because they don't understand what their teen is feeling. This can be especially true of parents of teens dealing with anxiety and depression. In *Why Is My Teenager Feeling Like This?*, Murray provides a remarkable resource for those parents. Thoroughly researched and filled with practical, biblical strategies, this is an absolute must-read for parents who want to help their struggling teen more effectively."

Jaquelle Crowe Ferris, Founder and COO, The Young Writer; author, *This Changes Everything*

"Parenting a teen who is riddled with anxiety or depression can be a daunting and overwhelming journey. Parents are often plagued by questions: *How did this happen? Did I cause this? Has God abandoned us?* In his compelling resource for parents, *Why Is My Teenager Feeling Like This?*, David Murray restores hope by providing both practical insight and meaningful strategies that promote healthy change. This is a must-read for parents navigating the darkness of depression or anxiety!"

Emilie DeYoung, Supervisor for Child and Adolescent Counseling, Family Wellness Center, Zeeland, Michigan

"With anxiety and depression at an all-time high in today's teens, this book could not come at a more crucial time. As someone who battled anxiety and depression as a teen and now navigates it with her own child, I found *Why Is My Teenager Feeling Like This?* to be an extremely practical, helpful, biblical, and hopeful book. Rather than giving spiritually cliché answers to a complex and multilayered issue, David Murray compassionately walks alongside hurting and overwhelmed parents, offering clarity, understanding, and wise counsel in how to better understand their teens' unique battles with anxiety and depression, as well as providing the practical and spiritual tools to support them through it. Whether you have a teen or want to prepare for the teen years, this book is a must-read. And you never know, you might even see yourself in these pages and find a path toward your own healing along the way."

Sarah Walton, coauthor, *Hope When It Hurts* and *Together through the Storms*

"This book has opened our eyes to the real nature of our son's struggle with anxiety and depression. It has helped us to communicate with him more effectively, empathize more lovingly, and turn our hearts from criticism to encouragement and understanding. It has made a difference in our relationship with our son, our family, and, most importantly, with Christ! The practical exercises not only helped our son but are also making an impact in our own lives as well. If you have a child who is fighting for hope, meaning, and relief from the death grip of anxiety and depression, we highly recommend this book!"

Layne and Tanya, parents of a teenager

"I wish I had this book when I first entered youth ministry. David Murray's discussion of who gets anxiety and depression, what causes these feelings, and what we can do to help teens we care about is compassionate, insightful, and tremendously helpful. His extensive list of tools to help teens toward healing is excellent, but his advice on how to partner with teens and how to walk alongside them in the process is what makes this book so valuable. *Why Is My Teenager Feeling Like This?* offered insights into my own moments of anxiety while also giving me practical wisdom for caring for teens."

Christopher Walker, Associate Pastor for Youth Ministry, Westminster Presbyterian Church, Lancaster Pennsylvania

"Whether you are unfamiliar or well-acquainted with anxiety and depression, David Murray's *Why Is My Teenager Feeling Like This?* will equip you with practical tools and theological truth as you shepherd your teen. I know I will return to this book when I'm anxious or when I need to support a loved one who is. Highly recommend it!"

Kristen Wetherell, author, *Fight Your Fears*; coauthor, *Hope When It Hurts*

"In these days of rising anxiety and depression, parents of teenagers need an accessible, empathetic, and wise guide. David Murray's books team up to provide parents and teens with a way to communicate hope and give grace to one another in these perplexing struggles. Pastors and youth workers will find in Murray a patient and seasoned coach in their efforts to care for anxious and depressed teens and their parents."

David Sunday, Lead Pastor, New Covenant Bible Church, St. Charles, Illinois

WHY IS MY TEENAGER FEELING LIKE THIS?

Other Crossway Books by David Murray

Exploring the Bible: A Bible Reading Plan for Kids

Exploring the Bible Together: A 52-Week Family Worship Plan

Meeting with Jesus: A Daily Bible Reading Plan for Kids

Refresh: Embracing a Grace-Paced Life in a World of Endless Demands with Shona Murray

Reset: Living a Grace-Paced Life in a Burnout Culture

Why Am I Feeling Like This? A Teen's Guide to Freedom from Anxiety and Depression

WHY IS MY TEENAGER FEELING LIKE THIS?

A Guide for Helping Teens through
Anxiety and Depression

David Murray

CROSSWAY®

WHEATON, ILLINOIS

Trade paperback ISBN: 978-1-4335-7075-9
ePub ISBN: 978-1-4335-7078-0
PDF ISBN: 978-1-4335-7076-6
Mobipocket ISBN: 978-1-4335-7077-3

Library of Congress Cataloging-in-Publication Data

Names: Murray, David, 1966 May 28– author. | Murray, David, 1966 May 28– Why am I feeling like this?

Title: Why is my teenager feeling like this? : a guide to helping teens through anxiety and depression / David Murray.

Description: Wheaton, Illinois : Crossway, 2020. | "To accompany Why am I feeling like this? a teen's guide to freedom from anxiety and depression." | Includes bibliographical references and index.

Identifiers: LCCN 2019047127 (print) | LCCN 2019047128 (ebook) | ISBN 9781433570759 (trade paperback) | ISBN 9781433570766 (pdf) | ISBN 9781433570773 (mobipocket) | ISBN 9781433570780 (epub)

Subjects: LCSH: Anxiety—Religious aspects—Christianity. | Depression, Mental—Religious aspects—Christianity. | Depression in adolescence—Religious aspects—Christianity. | Teenagers—Mental health. | Parent and teenager—Religious aspects—Christianity.

Classification: LCC BV4908.5 .M873 2020 (print) | LCC BV4908.5 (ebook) | DDC 248.8/45—dc23

LC record available at https://lccn.loc.gov/2019047127

LC ebook record available at https://lccn.loc.gov/2019047128

Crossway is a publishing ministry of Good News Publishers.

LB												
	30	29	28	27	26	25	24	23	22	21	20	
15	14	13	12	11	10	9	8	7	6	5	4	3	2	1

This book is dedicated to all Christians who give
their time and hearts to counseling struggling teens.
May God bless your faithful and loving service.

CONTENTS

Introduction

WHY IS MY TEENAGER FEELING LIKE THIS?

Why is my teenager feeling like this? Have you ever looked at your adolescent son or daughter and asked this question? You poured your life into your children. You provided for them in every way. You set them up for success. But now they are sinking. They can't get out of bed. They don't want to go to school. They can't function. They spend hours locked in their bedroom. They are nervous wrecks. This was not what you dreamed of. Instead of a confident, independent, happy, hopeful young man or woman, you now see a depressed, anxious, and empty soul.

Why is my teenager feeling like this? What went wrong? And what can I do about it? These are the questions that this book will answer. I wrote it to accompany *Why Am I Feeling Like This?: A Teen's Guide to Freedom from Anxiety and Depression*. As teens read that book, I hope parents (and teachers and pastors) will read this book alongside them. Rarely will teens recover from anxiety or depression without adult help. The adults closest to them have a vital role to play, and this guide will help parents and adult mentors minister to hurting teens.

Three Differences

This book differs from the teen book in three main ways. First, it provides more advanced information about teen anxiety and depression, the kind of information that would have made the teen book too long and complicated.

Second, it contains three extra sections at the beginning to help you understand anxiety and depression better: "Who Gets Anxiety and Depression?"; "What Causes Anxiety and Depression?"; and "What Can We Do About Anxiety and Depression?"

Third, and most importantly, this book gives spiritual encouragement and practical direction for parents and other adults who want to help but don't know what to do. It will show how much you can contribute, and how many resources for healing God has placed in the hands of his people. Yes, there is hope in the midst of despair.

Working Together

Apart from the extra sections at the beginning, the adult book follows the same structure as the teen book. This makes working together a lot easier. There is some overlapping content in the two books, maybe about 5 percent, but the vast majority of this book is new content tailored for parents and other adult mentors. You can therefore read this book as a stand-alone, but I recommend that you read the teen book as well if you want to provide the most help for your teen.

There are two ways of working with your teens. First, and ideally, you can do it in a structured way. You set up a time, say fifteen to thirty minutes every few days or every week, to discuss the book a chapter at a time, and go over the verses, prayers, and questions together. You can ask them to comment on what they learned from their book, and you can share what you learned from your book.

Although this is the ideal, as we know, teens don't always conform to ideals—which brings us to the second, more informal approach. You get both books and ask your teen to read his while you read yours. But you don't set up times and sessions for discussion. You simply try to understand and help your teen more casually and try to talk as opportunity arises. You will be growing in knowledge and usefulness as you read, but you are really at your teen's mercy as to how much input he allows you to give. His book encourages him to involve his parents or an adult mentor, so hopefully he will eventually drop his defenses and let you in.[1]

If he won't read his book or engage with you at all, it's going to be more difficult to make progress, but if you read both books, you'll be able to understand your teen better and also help him in practical and spiritual ways, perhaps without him realizing it.

Team Members

In addition to your own involvement, I encourage you to add other team members as finances and opportunity allow. For example, you might want to involve your doctor, your pastor, a Christian or biblical counselor, or a mental health professional. Depending on the severity of the depression or anxiety, your teen may need the more specialized help a doctor or another specialist can provide or put you in touch with. If you think your teen has suicidal thoughts, you must act immediately and get outside help. Look out for phrases such as:

"I want out."
"There's no reason to live."
"I'm done with life."
"I can't take the pain any longer."
"Everyone would be better off without me."

At the very worst, remember there is a National Suicide Prevention Lifeline, available twenty-four hours a day, every day: 1-800-273-TALK (8255).

Who Gets Anxiety and Depression?

If you are a parent of an anxious or depressed teen, you might feel as alone as your child does. Like your teen, you feel there's

---

1. You will notice that I have switched between male and female pronouns throughout the book, because what you learn will apply to both boys and girls.

no one else in this situation. You might even have decided you've failed as a parent. Why is my son or daughter like this when all my friends' kids are fine and flourishing? What have I done wrong?

If you're a pastor or teacher, you will have more experience of anxious teens, but you probably still feel confused about it. You can't figure it out. Sometimes the kids you least expect suffer in this way. Why? If we want to help our teens, we have to start by understanding who gets anxiety and depression.

TEEN ANXIETY AND DEPRESSION IS COMMON

Many anxious teens will feel as if they are completely weird, that no one else is like them or understands them. They look around at their peers and can't imagine anyone else their age feeling like they do. They see the carefully curated social media images of perfect, happy, and confident classmates and conclude that they are the odd one out. Ashamed and embarrassed, they withdraw from friends, family, and social occasions, to suffer alone in lonely isolation. "I'm just weird," they conclude.

One of the best things we can do for our teens is to explain to them that many teens suffer in the same way. Despite what the social media feeds communicate, the reality is that teen anxiety is at epidemic levels, so much so that it is now the most common issue for which teens seek counseling.

- Nearly a third of thirteen- to seventeen-year-olds will experience an anxiety disorder (38 percent of girls and 26 percent of boys).[2]
- An estimated six million American teens presently have some kind of anxiety disorder, although the number is probably higher because the majority do not seek treatment.[3]

2. "Anxiety Disorder Definitions," National Institute of Mental Health, 2017, https://www.nimh.nih.gov/health/statistics/any-anxiety-disorder.shtml.
3. Corrie Cutrer, "Why Are Our Children So Anxious?" *Christianity Today*, January 6, 2017, https://www.christianitytoday.com/women/2017/january/parenting-in-age-of-anxiety-children-teens.html.

- Fifty-four percent of college students surveyed said that they had "felt overwhelming anxiety" in the past twelve months.[4]
- In 2011, 11 percent of teen girls had a major depressive episode in the past year. By 2017, that number had risen to 20 percent.[5]
- While the depression rate for boys has risen more slowly, the suicide rate has spiked to a thirty-year high.[6]

Anecdotal evidence backs up the statistics. One female Christian counselor recently described how, when she first started counseling twenty-four years ago, "Probably one out of every twenty kids coming in were dealing with anxiety. . . . Now, out of my new appointments, I would say at least sixteen of every twenty families are here for that reason, if not more."[7]

It's not just common in our culture, it's also common in the Bible. Even strong and mature Bible characters such as King David and the Apostle Paul battled worry, anxiety, and fear (Ps. 56:3; 2 Cor. 7:5; 1:8). The most common command in the Bible is "Fear not!" which means it must be a very common problem.

TEEN ANXIETY AND DEPRESSION OFTEN COME TOGETHER

You might be wondering why one book would try to deal with both anxiety and depression. Aren't they different problems? While there are differences, many experts now view them as two sides of the one coin, or two faces of the one basic problem. Yes, someone can be depressed but not anxious, or anxious without being depressed, but about 50 percent of teens who have one also have the other, to some degree.

4. Greg Lukianoff and Jonathan Haidt, "The Coddling of the American Mind," *The Atlantic*, September 2015, https://www.theatlantic.com/magazine/archive/2015/09/the-coddling-of-the-american-mind/399356/.

5. "Major Depression," National Institute of Mental Health, February 2019, https://www.nimh.nih.gov/health/statistics/major-depression.shtml#part_155031.

6. Markham Heid, "Depression and Suicide Rates Are Rising Sharply in Young Americans, New Report Says. This May Be One Reason Why," *Time*, March 14, 2019, https://time.com/5550803/depression-suicide-rates-youth/.

7. Corrie Cutrer, "Why Are Our Children So Anxious?," *Christianity Today*, January 6, 2017, https://www.christianitytoday.com/women/2017/january/parenting-in-age-of-anxiety-children-teens.html.

When it comes to depression, 13 percent of twelve- to seventeen-year-olds experience major depression in any one year, with depression affecting about 20 percent of adolescents by the time they become adults. That's every fifth teen in your child's class.

We also find biblical figures who experienced depression. Look at how depressed the psalmists were in Psalms 32 and 88, how depressed Elijah was at the lowest point of his ministry (1 Kings 19:1–8), and how Job slipped into depression at various times (Job 3:11–15; 30:16–26).

As anxiety is more common than depression for teens, and it usually comes before depression, the primary focus of this book will be anxiety. However, most of the remedies work for both anxiety and depression, as we will see.

TEEN ANXIETY AND DEPRESSION ARE NORMAL

Apart from using statistics and the Bible to assure teens that anxiety and depression are common, one of the best ways we can "normalize" these problems is to talk about mental illness and other emotional disorders as common experiences in a fallen world. Speak about it around the supper table or in the car. If we are teachers or preachers, we can talk about it in the classroom, in the pulpit, or at youth groups. Look out for long-term changes in your teen's behavior and moods and take opportunities to ask her what's going on in her thoughts and feelings. You could say, for example, "You seem to be a bit down or troubled. Can I help in any way?" To maximize the chances of your teen opening up to you, try not to come across as judgmental, critical, or scared.

Only one thing is worse than never talking about such disorders, and that is to mock, shame, or stigmatize those who suffer with them. Such a cruel and arrogant attitude will ensure that our teens will never talk to us about these challenges or seek our help. They will either bottle it up and suffer in silence, or else they will seek help from others outside of the Christian community, who may lead them astray. At worst, they may start cutting themselves to find temporary relief, or even attempt suicide as a permanent solution.

Instead, in our homes, our schools, and our churches, we want to talk about these issues as normal abnormalities in an abnormal world. We want to build a culture of transparency and trust so that our teens will feel free and safe to talk about their fears without fear. Anxiety and depression are simply two of the many consequences of the fall, and teens should be able to talk about them just as we talk about asthma, broken arms, disrespect, purity, and so on.

TEEN ANXIETY AND DEPRESSION ARE VARIED

We must avoid stereotypes of anxiety and depression because they actually can manifest themselves in multiple ways. Just because we or someone else we know suffered in a certain way does not mean that everyone experiences it in that way.

There are many kinds of anxiety. The most common are panic disorder, specific phobias, generalized anxiety disorder, and social anxiety disorder.[8] Some anxiety (and depression) is genetic, sometimes it is a response to trauma, and sometimes it is caused by exhaustion or perfectionism. Some of these disorders are long-term but low-grade. Other times they are brief but acute. They make some kids withdraw and others aggressive. Sometimes it is the result of guilt—both true and false guilt. Nervous kids get it, but so do hyperconfident kids. Girls get it, and so do boys; although more girls admit it than boys. Help your teen identify their unique symptoms of anxiety—physical, spiritual, emotional, mental—so they can recognize it in the future.

It's important to appreciate the variety and diversity of anxiety and depression, because if we have a set but limited caricature of an anxious person, we could miss it or respond to it wrongly. This

8. "Anxiety Disorders," National Alliance on Mental Illness, March 2015, https://www.nami.org/NAMI/media/NAMI-Media/Images/FactSheets/Anxiety-Disorders-FS.pdf; "Anxiety Disorders," National Institute of Mental Health, July 2018, https://www.nimh.nih.gov/health/topics/anxiety-disorders/index.shtml; "Facts and Statistics," Anxiety and Depression Association of America, https://adaa.org/about-adaa/press-room/facts-statistics; "Symptom Checker," Child Mind Institute, 2019, https://childmind.org/symptomchecker/; "Anxiety Basics," Child Mind Institute, 2019, https://childmind.org/guide/anxiety-basics/.

is why it's important to get experienced professionals like doctors and trained counselors involved in diagnosing these disorders.

TEEN ANXIETY AND DEPRESSION ARE TERRIBLE

Imagine that you are driving your family to church, and you suddenly hit black ice, spin out of control, and start heading toward a precipice. Your fight-or-flight system is firing on all cylinders. You're sweating, your heart is pounding, your muscles are tensed, your insides are doing somersaults, and you know you are about to die.

But, by God's grace, your vehicle stops just before going over the cliff. You are safe but shaking uncontrollably; your guts are a mess, you can hardly string two words together, you want to cry or even scream.

That's what anxiety is like for many of our teens. You will calm down an hour or so after your brush with death, and eventually the memory of the black ice will fade. But for anxious teens, it's like they are heading toward the precipice twenty-four hours a day. That's how terrible and terrifying this can be for them. It's as horrifyingly real to them as you heading toward the cliff. Try to remember that when you are talking with them. Or look up the hashtag #thisiswhatanxietyfeelslike on Twitter to sample some of the raw descriptions that people have submitted.[9]

Depression is no better, and often is worse. Imagine the sadness you would feel if one of your loved ones died. That can be the level of pain in depression, often with no hope of alleviation. In 2016 the demographic with the highest increase in rate of suicide was ten- to fourteen-year-old girls, for whom the rate tripled.[10] Again, look up the hashtag #thisiswhatdepressionfeelslike for more graphic descriptions.

TEEN ANXIETY AND DEPRESSION ARE TREATABLE

One of the most encouraging aspects of teen anxiety is that although it is so common, varied, and terrible, it is also one of the

9. Also, see Sharon Horesh Bergquist, "How Stress Affects Your Body," TED-Ed video, October 22, 2015, YouTube, https://www.youtube.com/watch?v=v-t1Z5-oPtU.
10. "Suicide Rates Rising Across the U.S.," CDC website, June 7, 2018, https://www.cdc.gov/media/releases/2018/p0607-suicide-prevention.html.

most treatable mental or emotional disorders. That's why it's so tragic that a 2015 report from the Child Mind Institute found that only about 20 percent of young people with a diagnosable anxiety disorder get treatment.[11] Depression is more stubborn to remove, but, as this book will remind you, there's still much that can be done. God has provided many ways to heal these agonies or help your teen to manage and handle them better.

As parents, pastors, teachers, and counselors, we have a great opportunity to reach out to our suffering teens and help them access help, as well as play a role in providing help ourselves. One of the first steps in becoming a resource for our suffering teens is understanding what's actually happening in these disorders.

What Causes Anxiety and Depression?

When there's been a public tragedy like a building collapse or a flood, people often demand an investigation. The government responds by appointing an investigator to report on the causes of the disaster, a process that can take some time. Similarly, although we live in a day of instant fixes and we may be impatient to get to solutions for our teens, it's essential to pause in this chapter and consider the causes of anxiety and depression.

IDENTIFYING CAUSES IS IMPORTANT

Trying to identify the causes behind anxiety and depression is important for four reasons. First, *it relieves frustration*. You and your teen may be totally baffled as to why she feels the way she does. From the outside, her life looks fine. So why should her life be such a mess on the inside? It's frustrating because, as human beings, we are used to looking for a cause behind every effect. When we finally see it, we get it, we understand. Similarly, if we can find the causes of anxiety and depression, the frustration over what seemed to be irrational and mysterious will be reduced and relieved.

11. Susanna Schrobsdorff, "Teen Depression and Anxiety: Why the Kids Are Not Alright," *Time*, October 27, 2016, http://time.com/4547322/american-teens-anxious-depressed-overwhelmed/.

Second, *it increases sympathy*. When we can't figure out why our teens feel so bad, we can get impatient and critical of them. Are they just making it up? But when we identify a cause, we begin to understand why they may be feeling and acting in this way. They're not just imagining things. There's a real cause with a real effect. We then begin to feel much more sympathy.

Third, *it improves communication*. Ignorance, suspicion, frustration, and criticism shut down communication. Therefore, when we get knowledge, understanding, and sympathy, communication begins to flow again. Our teens feel accepted and loved and will trust us enough to talk to us without fearing rejection or condemnation. This is such a central element of healing for our teens.

Fourth, *it gets to the roots*. If we treat only symptoms, we will never provide deep and lasting healing. It's like chopping the top off garden weeds. They will grow back again eventually. But identifying and dealing with causes deals with the roots, and hopefully results in permanent removal and change.

IDENTIFYING CAUSES REQUIRES PATIENCE

The teen book is structured around stories of teen depression and anxiety. I deliberately chose the narrative approach there because it is the most likely to appeal to teens. They can identify with the characters and better engage with the material. The majority of this book is also structured around the same characters, although the content is intended to assist adults. However, because it can be helpful for adults to see the causes of anxiety and depression in a more systematic and tabulated form, I've provided the following table.

Causes can be divided into four main categories, but there are a number of causes in each of these categories. Therefore, it may take time to determine exactly where the anxiety or depression is coming from. There's a lot to explore, and often more than one cause is in play. But however long it takes, we must take time in this phase to ensure that we—and our teens—are not jumping to premature conclusions.

Causes of Anxiety and Depression

Spiritual Causes	• Wrong view of God or the gospel
	• Lack of Bible knowledge
	• Unbelief
	• Sin and unresolved guilt
	• Prayerlessness
	• Backsliding
	• Pornography
	• Discontent and ingratitude
	• Satanic attack
Physical Causes	• Malfunctioning biological system
	• Lack of exercise
	• Lack of rest and sleep
	• Poor diet
	• Abuse
	• Long-term stress and tension
	• Workaholism
Relational Causes	• Bullying
	• Identity theft
	• Perfectionism
	• Excessive expectations
	• Family breakdown
	• Conflict with parents
	• Friend drama
	• Bereavement
	• Social fear
Mental/Cognitive Causes	• Information overload
	• Social media
	• Overactive imagination
	• Unresolved problems
	• PTSD
	• False thinking patterns

I don't recommend sitting down with teens and interrogating them with this checklist of causes in your hand. It's better to engage in conversation with them, and ideally do more listening than talking. If they are reading their book, ask them if they identified with any of the characters, and maybe if there was more than one. Use this table more as a mental checklist.

Perhaps help them to keep an anxiety log for a few weeks, which records anxiety and depression occurrences—when and where, and what thoughts and feelings they had. Perhaps also record times of joy and peace. Then look for any patterns and lessons.

Anxious teens will often identify the physical causes first because so much of the experience of anxiety is physical. However, we need to explore the spiritual, relational, and cognitive or mental realms as well. While physical symptoms may be the primary manifestation of anxiety, the underlying causes will often be in one of the other realms. This is where involving a counselor with experience and skill is helpful, especially if you can't get your teen to talk to you.

IDENTIFYING CAUSES INVOLVES OPENNESS

If we come to people with our minds already made up about why they are anxious or why they should not be depressed, then we will not listen well or be sensitive to helpful hints in their words and actions. Our teen may have closed his mind to possibilities or be reluctant to talk about certain areas of his life. We will be more likely to get to the bottom of their issues if we all approach the problem with open minds. That means we must avoid assuming the problem is all spiritual, all physical, all mental, or all relational.

It also means we have to be aware that causes can come from more than one category. While I've tried to distinguish the four realms of causes, obviously there's overlap between them. God made us in such a way that our souls, bodies, thoughts, and feelings all affect each other. Indeed, in many cases a mixture of all four realms in different proportions is at the root of our teen's anxiety and depression. We must avoid oversimplifying.

IDENTIFYING CAUSES CAN BE PAINFUL

Sometimes a discussion of causes may reveal things that will bring us great pain as parents. We may uncover terrible sins or abuse in our teens' lives that shock and horrify us. We may discover that things we have done and said, or left undone and unsaid, have contributed to their suffering. Maybe we will see how our decisions or neglect have damaged our children. We might realize that our teens are actually not Christians after all and are desperately lost. We might have to face facts about ourselves and them that we have been trying to ignore or run away from.

If we are part of the problem, then confessing our sins to our teens and asking for forgiveness is an essential step in the process. We may not be to blame for everything, but insofar as we are, then we must take responsibility and follow the gospel pattern, however painful that may be to us. Our teens will never fully heal unless we truly confess and seek their forgiveness.

If we discover things we did not know before, such as bullying, pornography, self-harm, obsessive compulsive behavior, and so on, then it's important that we don't express shock, disgust, or self-pity. We must try to be unshockable and avoid turning the focus on ourselves.

Avoid language such as "I'm shocked at you"; "How could you do this to me?"; "I am so disappointed"; "If you were a Christian you wouldn't feel this or do this." If we want to be part of the solution, we need to keep the focus on their healing, not our offense or our disappointment. However painful it may feel to you, remember that their pain is far worse.

What Can We Do about Anxiety and Depression?

We've looked at who gets anxiety and depression and what causes them. We now want to consider the cures. Each case study in the teen book explains how God has provided various keys to unlock the chains of teen depression and anxiety. I previously tabulated the causes; here I do the same with the cures. The first column names the teen and their particular problem, the second identifies the cures in the form of keys, and the third summarizes the exercises that help to turn the key.

KEYS TO CURING ANXIETY AND DEPRESSION

Case	Key	Exercises
Introduction		• Circle the words that describe your thoughts and feelings.
1. Circular Sarah	The Key of Understanding	• Describe how anxiety and depression affect your thoughts, feelings, and body.
2. Tense Tom	The Key of Exercise	• Walk outside • Fitness app • Now-Here-This
3. Doomed Dave	The Key of Christ	• Categorize fears • Read a Gospel
4. Imaginative Imogen	The Key of Imagination	• Thought-stopping • Image therapy
5. Panicky Paul	The Key of Medication	• Six checkpoints on meds
6. Faithless Flavia	The Key of Scripture	• Daily Bible reading plan
7. Controlling Colin	The Key of Prayer	• Daily prayer • ACTS pattern • Thanksgiving journal
8. Depressed Dan	The Key of Elephant Training	• Psalm 77 therapy
9. Negative Nicole	The Key of Rethinking	• Identify false thoughts • Challenge false thoughts

KEYS TO CURING ANXIETY AND DEPRESSION

Case	Key	Exercises
10. Workaholic Will	The Key of Rest	• 4 x 4 breathing • Body scan
11. Beautiful Brianna	The Key of Identity	• Who am I? • Rebuild identity
12. Media Max	The Key of Digital Detox	• Digital detox questionnaire
13. Friendly Fiona	The Key of Christ's Friendship	• Friendship advice
14. Bullied Benton	The Key of Protection	• Cyberbullying solutions
15. Rebellious Rob	The Key of Respect	• Discussion with parents • Models of conflict resolution
16. Perfect Peyton	The Key of Realistic Expectations	• Self-counseling questions
17. Paralyzed Pam	The Key of Problem-Solving	• Work through challenging issue
18. Lonely Luke	The Key of Church	• Sunday project • Fear project • Service project

As with the causes, I haven't put this table of cures in the teen book because it might overwhelm our children. But for you, seeing the number of possible helps can be hope-giving and encouraging as you start out. And because teens need encouragement too, you can motivate them to join you on this journey in the following ways.

ENCOURAGE THEM THAT THEY HAVE ALREADY TAKEN A BIG STEP

If your teen is reading *Why Am I Feeling Like This?* he or she has already taken a big step on the path to recovery. As already noted, the vast majority of anxious and depressed teens do not seek or get help. It should give our teens great hope that they are already at this stage in the process. It means they have listened to their emotions and responded by seeking help.

ENCOURAGE THEM WITH THE NUMBER OF CURES

The chapters in both books look at each of the cures in more detail, but the table lets you see all the possible cures summarized in one place. This is to underline the range of remedies that God has so graciously provided. If you think it appropriate, use the table to remind your teen how lavish God has been in providing so many cures that are within their reach. If one doesn't work, there's no need to be discouraged. There are many more keys to try. But do note that some will be better for your teens than others, and you may need to experiment a bit.

ENCOURAGE THEM TO SEE THE BIG PICTURE

If they do look at the table of keys and feel overwhelmed, guide them back to the big picture in the causes table. There we see a simple four-part structure that holds everything together: spiritual, physical, relational, and mental. Or, more simply: soul, body, relationships, mind. We want to train our teens to think about themselves and their problems using this simple four-part holistic framework.

ENCOURAGE THEM TO GET STARTED

Talking is easy, but we have to start doing. So come alongside them and support them as they take the first steps toward peace and joy. Remind them to prioritize reading their book and doing the exercises, because anxiety and depression can get worse if untreated, making them harder to dislodge.

ENCOURAGE THEM TO TAKE A STEP AT A TIME

It's never a good idea to attempt too much at one time. Try to judge your teen's capacity and pace the book accordingly. It might be an idea to take a few days or a week to process and think about each chapter. Only when it's been absorbed should your teen move on to the next chapter. Alternatively, you could read the whole book together and then decide which three keys to focus on. The goal must be to make it manageable and doable.

ENCOURAGE THEM TO TURN THE KEY

At the end of each chapter of the teen book is a section called Turning the Key. Usually it includes a memory verse, a couple of questions or exercises, and a prayer. Rally your teen to learn the verse and answer the questions or do the exercises. We must help our teens to move from theory to practice and to learn new habits and skills for the future. That's what the keys are designed to do—build habits that will not only cure but also prevent reoccurrence. I've put more exercises in the adult book than in the teen book, because I wanted to keep things as simple as possible for the teens. At whyamIfeelinglikethis.com, you'll find more detailed videos and exercises that will also move theory into practice. We must be patient with our teens; the more they practice with these keys, the more progress they will make.

ENCOURAGE THEM TO WORK WITH YOU

Earlier we talked a little about the importance of working together if possible. Apart from making yourself available to answer questions, arrange set times each week or two when you will sit down with your teen and chat about what he or she has been learning. Use questions like:

- What did you find helpful in this chapter?
- What did you disagree with?
- What did you not understand?
- What did you do as a result of reading this chapter?
- What are you planning to do differently?
- How can I help you put this into practice?

Try to build a relationship that not only provides accountability but also support and sympathy.

ENCOURAGE THEM WITH YOUR OWN LESSONS

Remind your teen that although you may not have an anxiety disorder or depression, you do get anxious or sad from time to time. Share how the book is helping you to deal with your own emotional and mental distress. Show that you are also a struggler and you need and receive help too.

ENCOURAGE THEM THAT YOU WILL STAY WITH THEM

While expressing confidence in your teen that he or she can do this with God's help, we also need to be realistic. Sometimes our teens will forget or fail to read the chapter or do the exercises. Sometimes they will go back to old habits. Tell them that you expect this to happen from time to time, but you will stick with them. You will not give up on them. You are in this for the long haul.

ENCOURAGE THEM TO PRAY

Hopefully you already pray with your teens, but it's especially critical to do so as you work through the books together. Make sure you pray with them before and after each discussion session and ask God to deepen the lessons learned and make them permanent. But encourage them to also pray for themselves. I've provided prayers at the end of each chapter that they can use. But they can also make up their own prayers. Remind them that God hears their cries and blesses the means of healing that he has provided.

ENCOURAGE THEM WITH GROWTH

Overcoming anxiety and depression builds resilience and other character traits for future challenges (Rom. 5:3–5). If we can view this as an opportunity to learn rather than a disaster to avoid, we will help our teens see this painful experience as a special school with its own special lessons, which will often prepare them for life better than overprotecting them usually does.

1

CIRCULAR SARAH

Sarah was overwhelmed in her junior year by the pressure of being behind in her studies, upcoming exams, her school soccer schedule, and criticism from her older teammates. Feeling unwanted on her soccer team, she couldn't stop thinking about what she imagined the other girls thought and said about her. Eventually the vicious cycle of unstoppable thoughts affected her sleep, leaving her feeling exhausted, sick, fearful, and worried that she might be going crazy.

The Key of Understanding

As Sarah demonstrates, one of the most horrible aspects of anxiety and depression is the feeling of being out of control. The experience is disorienting and confusing, chaotic and disorderly. Teens feel as if they're being sucked into a vortex they cannot resist. That sense of being a passive victim, of having no control over these malevolent forces, is one of the most terrifying and paralyzing features of anxiety and depression.

Sarah's healing began when she was helped to understand the *worry > anxiety > stress cycle*. Although it doesn't feel like it at the time, there usually is a predictable order to anxiety. Helping our teens understand the normal process of anxiety can help prevent anxiety attacks, equip them to handle them better, and reduce their length and intensity. Let's look at the *worry > anxiety > stress cycle* and then consider the connection to depression.

WORRY

We must start by saying that worry and fear can be a good thing . . . in short and small doses. Our kids need a degree of worry if they are to successfully study for exams or avoid dangerous behavior. Good worry enables them to anticipate a potential problem and plan to avoid it or overcome it. Good worry comes at the right time and to the right degree to motivate right actions. Worry is natural in teens because they are moving from childhood to adulthood and encountering lots of new information and new challenges in themselves and in their lives.

Unless we help our teens understand and accept a degree of worry at certain times, they are going to become worried about every experience of worry. One of the most essential parenting skills is learning how to gradually expose our children to increasingly challenging situations that teach them to view fear and worry as appropriate and helpful, and build resilience for future challenges.[1] In contrast, anxious overparenting will often make our kids more anxious and unable to face difficulties in life.

Although worry can be good, worry can also be bad. Worry is a bad thing when it becomes a big thing or a constant thing, or when it is out of proportion to the problem or obstacle. It is a bad thing if it predicts problems or obstacles that are never likely to occur. It is a bad thing if it leads to excessive anxiety, the second step in the *worry > anxiety > stress cycle*.

ANXIETY

After worrying *thoughts* come anxious *feelings*. If it's good worry, the anxious feelings are also good. They help to motivate our kids and heighten their performance. Appropriate worry and anxiety before an exam or a sporting competition help our kids to focus and raise their game. The normal human stress

---

1. See Greg Lukianoff and Jonathan Haidt, *The Coddling of the American Mind* (New York: Penguin, 2019) for more on overprotecting children from risks, ideas, and the uncomfortable.

response, sometimes called the fight-or-flight response, that God designed for our good injects extra adrenaline and cortisol into their systems, enhancing their senses, strength, concentration, and responses.

But if it's bad worry—if it's excessive and goes on too long—then bad anxiety is the result. Instead of helping, it hinders. Instead of improving performance, our kids end up paralyzed, panicky, or obsessive. When they think of the next test, the feelings of fear, dread, and terror overwhelm them and dominate their whole lives. It becomes obsessive, so that they cannot stop thinking about it. This may result in compulsive behavior and repetitive rituals connected with counting, cleaning, or checking things.

Sometimes it accelerates into a full-blown panic attack. The fight-or-flight system that was designed to be limited, brief, and rare switches on to sustained high alert with many damaging consequences.

Some teens, though, skip the worry stage and just go straight to anxiety. If we were to ask them, "Why are you worried or anxious?" they would reply, "I have no idea. I'm not thinking about anything in particular, I'm just always jumpy and anxious." They have a general anxiety, to one degree or another.

Whether the anxiety is specific or general, all this overactivity in their thoughts and feelings, all this worry and anxiety, often impacts their bodies in the form of stress.

STRESS

If worry takes place in the *thoughts*, and anxiety in the *feelings*, stress is what results in the *body*. Worried thoughts and anxious feelings multiply to produce frightening bodily effects: heart racing or pounding, breathlessness, headaches, trembling, tension, dizziness, cold sweats, twitching, stomach cramps, nausea, exhaustion, restlessness, insomnia, tightness in the chest or throat, and so on.

This then starts a never-ending loop because our kids start worrying about these physical symptoms. "Am I seriously ill? Am

I going to die? Am I going mad?" Which, of course, creates more anxiety and more stress, and so the *worry > anxiety > stress cycle* continues. They then feel ashamed and angry and may respond by avoiding people or places, resorting to alcohol or drugs, self-harm, and even thoughts of suicide.

Depression

Not surprisingly, once a teen has been through the *worry > anxiety > stress cycle* a few times, or is stuck in it, exhaustion and a sense of hopelessness set in, creating the ideal conditions for depression to join the cycle. Anxiety is mentally, emotionally, and spiritually exhausting, draining lives of joy and filling them with despair. Kids eventually give up fighting, and then depression adds its voice to the *worry > anxiety > stress cycle*.

But it doesn't always go that way. You can be depressed without being anxious and vice versa. Sometimes depression comes before anxiety, especially if a person has experienced serious illness, bereavement, trauma, or other painful events. Sadness and darkness overwhelm us, resulting in sleep problems, eating issues, confusion, indecisiveness, and a general sense of worthlessness and hopelessness. This often starts off the *worry > anxiety > stress cycle*, plunging the depressed person into an even deeper hole.

TURNING THE KEY

The teen book has a number of exercises and questions at the end of each chapter. Ideally, you want to work through these with your teen or at least informally help him or her as follows.[2]

1. *The Wave.* When your teen gets into the *worry > anxiety > stress cycle*, say to him, "We know what's happening now. We understand it. Remember when you were young, and you saw a big wave coming when you were in the ocean? You were so scared at first because you didn't know what was going to happen. But after a few waves passed, you learned to brace yourself, take a deep breath, feel the wave lifting you up and then lowering you down as it passed. Then you could relax again. Let's view anxiety like that. Don't fight it, just let it pass through."

2. *The Roller Coaster.* Use the roller coaster illustration to help them view their emotions more objectively. When their emotions start carrying them away, say to them, "Get off the roller coaster of your feelings and watch the ups and downs instead." By doing so, we are trying to help them view their feelings as a spectator rather than a participant. This helps to cool the emotions and view the experience more rationally and calmly.

3. *Labeling.* During or after an episode of anxiety, walk through the *worry > anxiety > stress cycle* with them. The exercise in their book asks them to describe how the experience impacts their thoughts, feelings, and body. Help them identify the sequence and label the thoughts. This labeling will give them a sense of control and reduce the power of their thoughts and feelings.

4. *The Box.* When they are ruminating over things people said to them, help them to visualize a box that they put the comment in, tape it up, and file on a shelf with a sign on it: "Danger: Do Not Open."

5. *Schedule.* One of the causes of Sarah's anxiety was overscheduling and overcommitment. Consider whether your teen is too busy and overcommitted, and needs to cut back in order to reduce the general pressure upon her.

6. *Connection.* Try to identify how much depression is in the mix and how it is connected to anxiety.

---

2. You will find extra exercises throughout this book that are not included in the teen book.

2

TENSE TOM

Tom found it impossible to relax. He was tense and uptight all the time, giving him headaches, back pain, and overall stiffness, and making it difficult for him to get to sleep. A part of the problem was lack of exercise. He was sitting down for most of the day at school, in his car, and at his bedroom desk. But there was also the nonstop worry about his mom's cancer and the side effects of her chemotherapy. Tom's pastor could see how stressed Tom was and counseled him to trust God with his mom and memorize some comforting Scriptures. But he also advised him to see his doctor.

The Key of Exercise

One of the best things we can do for anxious or depressed teens is to get them exercising. Everyone I know who's made progress in overcoming anxiety and depression has found exercise to be a key component of any package of recovery. That's why Tom's doctor prescribed a five-step plan for him (see teen book): (1) using a stand-up desk, (2) walking outside, (3) lifting light weights (4) engaging in sports and hobbies, and (5) eating healthy. What can we do to assist our teens in this?

BELIEVE THE BIBLE

Obviously, the Bible was never intended to be a guide to exercise or diet. It does, however, contain some important general principles about the connection between the body, the mind, and the emotions. Look, for example, at the impact of guilt upon the psalmist's physical health (Pss. 32; 38; 51). Then there's Solomon's teaching on the interaction between healthy emotions and healthy bodies (Prov. 17:22). The book of Job further demonstrates how much physical illness impacts moods. The Bible teaches that the physical, the emotional, the mental, and the spiritual are all tied together in our humanity.

The Bible also teaches us to steward our bodies, not just our souls, for God's glory. The bodies of believers are for the Lord, members of Christ, temples of the Holy Spirit, God's property, and bought with a price (1 Cor. 6:13–20). Therefore we are to glorify God with our bodies (6:20), which means educating ourselves about them and caring for them.

READ THE SCIENCE

While the Bible teaches us the general principle that bodily health influences spiritual and emotional health, and vice versa, and that we are accountable to God for how we steward our bodies, science can supply us with many of the details of how these connections work and how to care for our bodies.

If there's one thing that science is loud and clear on, it's that sedentary lifestyles are a major contributory factor to emotional disorders. Young bodies especially need to move and exercise. There are plenty of articles about this on reliable websites. Do a quick Google search or look at whyamIfeelinglikethis.com for links to the latest research. Why not pick out some that are written at a more popular level to share with your teen and start a conversation about the importance of exercise for healthy emotions?

BUY A STAND-UP DESK

If your teen is spending hours sitting at a desk every day (and most teens are), then buy a stand-up desk so he can do some of his studying standing up. The usual recommendation is to do an hour standing up for every hour sitting down. It takes a few days to get used to, but the health benefits will soon be obvious. It will actually improve your teen's studying as well. You can buy relatively inexpensive desk-toppers, which sit on top of a normal desk and can be raised up and down as necessary. If you need further motivation, do an internet search for infographics on "sitting disease."

ENCOURAGE EXERCISE

Although you could buy a treadmill or elliptical to get your teen started, there are many benefits of exercising outside in the fresh air and sunlight, and that should be the aim. Perhaps you can go hiking together from time to time.

In some places, exercising outside is not possible at certain times of year. You could buy your teen a gym membership and new athletic gear to boost her motivation. This is all money well spent, and it can be more effective than hours of counseling or bottles of meds. You still want to encourage your teen to walk outside whenever possible—ideally without the phone and earbuds.

If you can afford it, consulting a reliable personal trainer can be a good starting point. Not only do trainers tailor exercise programs for individuals; they also provide some outside accountability and motivation.

If your child is resistant to exercise, remember that even stretching exercises can help remove stress chemicals and stimulate good chemicals, as well as relax the body. The good thing about stretches is that they can be done just about anywhere.

DEPRESSURIZE

Although we need to encourage our teens to exercise, we don't want to make exercise another massive pressure in their life. One of the reasons some kids are stressed out is because many parents push their kids hard all year round on a wide range of competitive sports. Early morning practices, travel, evening games, and the drama surrounding these activities are huge stressors on our kids. Once football or soccer season is over, it's straight into basketball, then it's track, then baseball and softball, and on and on it goes.

The result is that sport is no longer a joy, but another "to-do." Sports have become so overorganized, overcompetitive, and over-pressurized that they are a drainer rather than a filler. We need to let our kids learn to play again. Pick-up basketball and soccer are often far more therapeutic than official organized sports. Why not limit them to one season of an organized sport a year so that the pressure is temporary and limited rather than year-round. Their bodies will benefit as well as their emotions.[1]

PROVIDE HEALTHY FOOD

A lot of our teens are going to school with little or no breakfast, then fast-fooding and snacking throughout the day. This is bad for their metabolism as well as their mental health. Help them to start the day with a good healthy breakfast such as scrambled eggs and toast, or oatmeal, fruit, and a protein yogurt. Provide lunches for them to eat at school that are healthy and tasty. Cook homemade food with as few processed ingredients as possible. Keep the meals balanced.

All this is going to cost more than junk food. But if it prevents or improves junk moods, is that not a price worth paying? Although it's difficult to change eating habits, science can help us here in terms of information and motivation. For example, caffeine, refined white sugar, artificial sweeteners, and soda have been found to increase anxiety, whereas chicken, brown rice, tuna, oats, yogurt, avocados, bananas, and whole grains have been found to help. Consult a nutritionist or dietician for up-to-date information and advice.

IDENTIFY EATING DISORDERS

Sometimes eating disorders accompany anxiety and depression. This is a very serious and difficult problem that requires profes-

1. See Peter Gray, "The Decline of Play," TEDx talk, June 13, 2014, YouTube, https://www.youtube.com/watch?v=Bg-GEzM7iTk.

sional intervention and Christian input. If you are worried that your teen is going down this road, try to gain some understanding about the problem before you start a conversation with him or her.

As for professional intervention, it's vital that you get expert help promptly, because the situation can become very serious very fast. Start with your doctor and seek a referral to a specialist. Although your teen will likely fight against any intervention, it is our right and duty as parents to protect our children from themselves.

Usually, by the time you notice your teen has an eating disorder, many false ideas and beliefs have taken root in her mind and heart. You will want to read Christian literature on the subject and involve your pastor or a counselor with a Christian worldview to work on slowly and compassionately identifying and replacing these falsehoods with truth.

TURNING THE KEY

There were some things that Tom's doctor could not change, such as his mom's cancer and chemo. However, the things Tom could work on, such as diet and exercise, helped him cope with his mom's situation and handle it much better. The relaxation techniques his pastor taught him also helped.

1. *Exercise*. Encourage regular daily unpressurized exercise, starting with a walk outside and then adding light or medium weights either at home or a local gym. A personal trainer or reputable YouTube videos can provide some structure to this. We don't want teens pushing themselves to their limits. The ideal exercise intensity for mental and emotional health is 40 percent of a person's physical limits.

2. *Break*. Give them a break from year-round organized competitive sports. Instead, help them to pursue relaxing and renewing hobbies and pastimes in various seasons of the year.

3. *Apps*. Apps like MyFitnessPal can help with education and accountability for exercise and diet. Research which foods help to lower stress, and which ones increase it.

4. *Now-Here-This*. When your teen's mind is racing and his body is tensing up, help him relax and unwind by using the *Now-Here-This* technique to focus on the present moment (now, not the past or future), his present environment (here, not any other place), and his present senses (what his is currently seeing, hearing, etc.). Do this out loud with him until it becomes more of an automatic or habitual response for him when he is getting stressed. You can even build it into the days when your teen is not stressed, to keep him in a general state of calm.

5. *TV Channels*. Use this TV channel illustration. Imagine a TV with three channels: channel 1 is the past; channel 2, is the present; and channel 3 is the future. Urge them keep their mind on channel 2.

6. *The Next Five*. Keep the focus on what needs to be done in the next five minutes. What do you need to do right now? Then do that with focus.

3

DOOMED DAVE

Doomed Dave was me. I suffered with spiritual anxiety in my teens because I was living a sinful life. I was not right with God, and I knew if I died I would go to hell. Although I was enjoying some successes, I was living under a dark cloud of fear, especially when I heard convicting sermons. By my early twenties, I had gone even deeper into sin, and sometimes I was too scared to sleep. In God's sovereign mercy, he saved me in my early twenties after a particularly unhappy year. I not only knew my sins were forgiven by Christ, but I experienced unforgettable peace and joy.

The Key of Christ

In the last two chapters we've looked at how some depression and anxiety can be traced to the body and the mind. Now, we zoom in on Jesus Christ and the specific ways in which he can bring peace to anxious souls. Here are some general lessons about the spiritual causes and cures of anxiety and depression.

YOUR TEEN MAY NOT BE CONVERTED

We may not like to face this truth, but we have to admit up front that our teen's anxiety may, at least partly, be because he or she is not a believer. Yes, your child may go to church, say she is a Christian, talk Christian language, and do Christian things; but she may not know Christ personally. She may not even understand the gospel.

That's why we must make teens think about their spiritual state. If they are not believers in Christ, we actually want them to have anxiety—we want them to be afraid to some extent because they are in a perilous spiritual condition. The aim is not to terrorize them but to use a degree of spiritual fear to motivate them to seek and find Jesus for their salvation and their peace.

Although challenging them here may cause a temporary upswing in their anxiety, addressing this issue may ultimately be the cure of their anxiety. It's better that they experience temporary anxiety than eternal anxiety.

A lot more anxiety than we think is actually caused by our teens not truly understanding the gospel, or not really knowing Christ. Where there is unresolved guilt, where there is an underlying sense that they are not right with God, where they haven't grasped the gospel, all of that is fertile ground for fear and discouragement.

YOUR TEEN NEEDS TO KNOW JESUS PERSONALLY

The ultimate aim is to help our teens grasp the reality and value of Jesus, to draw them to him, to stimulate desire for him, to make him a real living person in their lives. Use my testimony in the teen book to talk your teens through all that Jesus can give to them: forgiveness instead of guilt, perfection instead of failure, purpose instead of aimlessness, contentment instead of greed, obedience rather than rebellion. Show them the diversity and range of his work. It's not enough for them to know God generally. They must know Jesus specifically.

Try to show this in your own life too. Bring Jesus into everyday conversation, demonstrate how real he is in your life, and highlight how varied and versatile his work is. Explain how he came to secure peace not only between us and God objectively, but in our own hearts subjectively.

It's not enough just to know *about* Jesus; they have to know Jesus personally. Explain to them what saving faith is, how it involves abandoning all other hopes and grounds of acceptance, and trusts in Jesus totally and exclusively. Remind them that he is the way, the truth, and the life. He gives peace that the world cannot give. He came that we might have life. He came to remove condemnation and to reconcile us to God.

YOUR TEEN NEEDS TO HEAR
THE GOSPEL AGAIN AND AGAIN

Even if your teen is a Christian and has evidenced real understanding of the gospel, don't assume that he has a present hold of the gospel. The devil is an expert at creating gospel amnesia. Even Christian teens need to be reminded again and again that they are saved by grace through faith alone in Christ alone. They especially need help to grasp that no matter their feelings or their sins, they are accepted in Christ. On good days and bad days, Christ is the same. When they are unfaithful, he is faithful. When they are rejected by others, he accepts them. When they are hated, Jesus loves them. When they are condemned, he justifies them. Preach the gospel to them Monday through Saturday as well as Sunday.

YOUR TEEN NEEDS TO FOLLOW
JESUS WHOLEHEARTEDLY

Some of the most anxious people I've known are backslidden Christians. They don't have either the false peace of the world or the true peace of Christ. They are miserable in their sin and spiritual coldness. They are trying to have the world and Christ, the "best" of both worlds, but they end up with the worst of both worlds. They don't enjoy peace with God, but neither can they enjoy this world, because of their guilty consciences.

That's why we want to encourage our teens to be all-in for Christ. The more devoted they are to Christ's kingdom, the more obedient they are to Christ's commandments, the more submissive they are to Christ's plan for them, the more of Christ's glory they seek to promote, then the more inner peace they will enjoy. They may suffer outwardly because of their wholehearted commitment to Christ, but they will have an inner peace and joy that the world cannot give or take away.

YOUR TEEN CAN BE ASSURED OF A SYMPATHETIC EAR

One of the most peace-giving truths is that Jesus is touched with the feelings of our weaknesses, including the infirmity of anxiety, fear, worry, and stress (Heb. 4:15). In his case, it was justified and sinless, but it was still real. Teens can therefore approach him boldly, without embarrassment, and pour out their hearts to him knowing that he knows, understands, sympathizes, and wants to support them. He's not only been a teen himself; he's also experienced deep and agonizing emotional distress. Indeed, he knew it to a far greater degree than anyone else ever did. Christ understands human sufferings and can perfectly sympathize with us, far better than even the best earthly counselor. That's why Isaiah calls him the "Wonderful Counselor" and "Prince of Peace" (Isa. 9:6).

YOUR TEEN NEEDS TO BE REMINDED OF HEAVEN

If we use all the means God has graciously provided, we will find that anxiety, from whatever causes, can be significantly and sufficiently reduced, and even totally removed in some cases. However, whatever the degree of healing God is pleased to give, we need to remind even the young that however long we live on earth, it is a very short time compared to the length and quality of eternal peace. That's why Paul urges us to consider that the sufferings of this present time are not worthy to be compared with the glory that is to be revealed (Rom. 8:18). Remind your Christian teen that even if God leaves some anxiety in his life, it will be more than compensated for by the peace that he will enjoy forever in heaven. It will make current anxieties look like a tiny dot on the horizon.

TURNING THE KEY

1. *Categorize.* Guide your teen to think through where his or her various anxieties are coming from. Use the following categories:

- *Physical:* Fear of illness, disease, or of being physically hurt.
- *Social:* Fear of social situations or of what people think or say about him.
- *Spiritual:* Fear of death, fear of punishment for sin, fear about being a hypocrite.
- *Psychological:* Fears that are generated by the mind, often imaginary or exaggerated.

Do the same categorization with any sadness in his life.

2. *Pastor.* If even some of your teen's anxiety or depression is spiritual, try to involve your pastor or an experienced Christian that you trust as a spiritual guide.

3. *Positive.* Show teens the positive side of Christianity, all that they can have and enjoy as a Christian: the peace and joy of forgiveness, perfection, purpose, contentment, and obedience. Read a Gospel with them and keep their focus on Christ rather than on Christians or the church.

4. *Gospel basics.* Keep the basics of the gospel before your teen at all times in Bible reading, prayer, and everyday conversation.

5. *Priorities.* Jesus's sermon on anxiety (Matt. 6:25–32) was sandwiched between two verses on serving and seeking God's kingdom first (6:24, 33). Getting our priorities right is one of the cures.

4

IMAGINATIVE IMOGEN

Imogen was blessed with a vivid imagination, but it became a curse to her because of her fatal attraction to bad news stories. She would read about things like school shootings and other tragedies and imagine herself in these awful scenarios. She would mentally rerun all the scary movies she had seen. Always thinking the worst was going to happen, she was often fearful and sad.

The Key of Imagination

If you could see inside your teen's brain, you would see a cinema with a movie on an endless loop. In many cases, it's an R-rated film containing terrifying and disturbing images of pain and disaster.

Some teens watch movies they themselves have directed and produced. They have chosen to fill their minds with certain images and to watch the same movie every day. Some have reels of past trauma that they run, others are more taken up with present images, and others are more futuristic as they anticipate various disasters waiting to happen.

Some teens reluctantly watch movies that others have directed and produced. They've experienced bullying and abuse, and detailed visual memories of these incidents flood their minds and hearts, often every day, and sometimes many times a day. It doesn't take much of a trigger to press *Play* again.

Whoever it is that directed and produced the movie, the impact of watching it is the same—worry, pain, and stress. Why are such images so powerful and influential?

VISUAL CREATURES

God has made us in such a way that we are attracted to images, scenes, graphics, and pictures, and they imprint themselves on our minds more vividly than mere words. That's why God made such a beautiful visual feast in the garden of Eden. Sin, however, entered the picture and our imaginations with the result that sinful and harmful images now flood our minds, and our teens especially find it difficult to stop them.

In Matthew 6:25–34, Jesus described what he saw when he looked inside the minds of those around him—a constant loop of worrying images about what to eat, what to drink, and what to put on. These were just samples of the kinds of movies that run in the heads of all people. And it's not just worrying images; there are often also sad images that result in depression.

In the teen book, I've highlighted the most popular teen "movies" such as the perfectionistic standards we impose on them, Instagram, trauma, bullies, an angry God, violent media, and so on. Round and round and round these "videos" go. It's a mental torture, like being chained to a seat in a cinema as some of the scariest images and sounds play again and again. That's what a teen's brain often looks like.

We can try telling our teens to stop this. But no matter how hard they press *Stop*, the images keep coming. That's because they can't stop something without starting something else. Instead of trying to stop bad images, they have to replace them with good images, with good "movies." That's what Jesus trained people to do in Matthew 6. And that's how we can help our teens.

WHAT ARE THEY WATCHING?

The first step is to find out what they are watching. When you see your teen stressing out, ask her, "What are you seeing? What picture are you viewing in your mind?" Talk to her about how that picture got in there and how it is affecting her. Identifying and naming the troubling image is vital because often our teens are not aware they are doing this. Use the image of a cinema to help them visualize and see what they are doing.

Second, take them to Matthew 6:25–34 and show them how the answer is not to stop imagining, but to do better imagining, to replace bad images with good. Then show them the two primary sources for new and better images to feast upon—natural images and supernatural images.

NATURAL IMAGES

I cannot emphasize enough how important this is. We can get our teens outside their own heads by getting them outside. If they spend their days indoors just looking at their devices, they are going to fill their minds with the worst kinds of images. As Jesus pointed to the birds of the air and the flowers of the field, we need to point our teens to the amazing wonders of God's creation and providence all around us. There are so many different scenes just waiting to be discovered and enjoyed.

Get them a telescope and point them to the stars and planets. Buy them binoculars and point them to the birds. Provide a microscope and show them the minutiae of God's creation. Encourage them to snorkel and look at all that is under the sea. Put them out in the garden to work, seeing beauty in the flowers and goodness in vegetables. Take them to a zoo to see the animals. Purchase a quality camera and lens for them, maybe sign them up for photography lessons, and encourage them to take pictures of what they see. Give them a fishing rod to go catch fish. Take them out in a boat. Go camping or skiing. Just get them outside and fill their eyes, ears, and noses with the sense-ational feasts God has surrounded us with.

The aim is not only to see nature, but to see God in nature, to see God's wisdom, beauty, power, and glory in what he has made. As Jesus did, highlight his care and providence for much less important things such as birds and fields, in order to encourage teens that he'll also look after them.

SUPERNATURAL IMAGES

God has also provided multiple pictures in his word as well as his world. The Bible is not a dry book of dusty laws, but a unique photo album displaying 3-D pictures of God and his truth. For the teens, I highlighted a number of images that God uses to teach his people about himself (king, father, shepherd, shield, etc.). But these are just samples of the multiple graphics God has painted in his word for us to discover and enjoy.

As you read the Bible with your teen, look out for images of God and his people. Encourage your teen to do the same and to watch for images in sermons too. Keep reminding him of how God uses pictures to teach us, to replace harmful images of our own and others' making, and to heal us. In doing so, you will help direct and produce a new film to run on your teen's internal screen. And your teen will leave that cinema of image therapy with more happiness and peace as a result.

TURNING THE KEY

1. *Study.* Read Matthew 6:25–34 with your teen. Highlight how Jesus cares for people whose emotions are causing them problems and that he lovingly provides wise solutions.

2. *Identify images.* Help teens identify what images they are viewing (from their minds, movies, games, etc.) and how they influence their thoughts and feelings. A Stress in America report found that immigration, sexual assault, and, above all, school shootings were fueling stress among fifteen- to twenty-one-year olds.[1]

3. *Replace images.* Show what images Jesus wants us to fill our minds with—images from nature and the Bible—and how these are designed to change our thoughts and feelings.

4. *Nature trips.* Encourage trips in and exploration of nature, and use all the senses to carve deep impressions on our imaginations that can be recalled at other times. If your teen can't walk in nature due to weather or other obstacles, view nature photos or documentaries that you can find online.

5. *Visualization.* Get them to visualize scenes in their minds—scenes of them laughing or on vacation or practicing their hobby or being with friends, and notice how that changes their feelings.

1. "APA Stress in America™ Survey: Generation Z Stressed About Issues in the News but Least Likely to Vote," American Psychological Association, October 30, 2018, https://www.apa.org/news/press/releases/2018/10/generation-z-stressed.

5

PANICKY PAUL

Although Paul was raised by godly parents and can't remember a time when he didn't love the Lord Jesus, in his midteens he started struggling with fear and despondency. After a few months of this, he started suffering with panic attacks. As praying and reading the Bible more didn't help, he worried he might not be a Christian. Eventually he told his mom, who shared that she had similar experiences as a teen, and that many members of her family had depression and anxiety. She encouraged him to see the family doctor about medication because it had helped her recover, but Paul was reluctant because he thought Christians shouldn't be on medication for anxiety and depression. .

The Key of Medication

Most of us have been involved in car accidents or come very close to being in them. Do you remember what happened when you realized the danger you were in? Do you remember the panic, the fear, the stimulation of your senses, the rapid reactions, the bracing of yourself, and so on?

What you experienced was the fight-or-flight system. We looked at this when we considered circular Sarah, but we need to look at it in a bit more detail here. This stress-response system is a gift of God that helps to motivate and energize us when we face stresses (such as exams) or danger (such as a threat to our lives). It tells our body to pump the chemicals cortisol and adrenaline into our systems, which speed up our thinking, reduce our reaction times, strengthen our muscles, heighten our senses, and thicken our blood. This helps us to rise to the occasion of stresses like exams, fight off or get out of danger, minimize the damage, and slow down any bleeding.

Usually our fight-or-flight system turns off when the stress or danger has passed, and we go back to normal. We don't want to live in a permanent state of fight-or-flight. However, for some people, their fight-or-flight system malfunctions and turns on when there is no danger. For others, it turns on for some traumatic event, or a series of traumatic events, and won't return to normal. There's nothing they can do about it. It's not a decision or a lack of faith. It's a physical biological problem that leaves them in a state of anxiety that they cannot control.

If it goes on too long, eventually the person is worn out, and depression sets in. It's similar to what would happen to a car if we revved it up too high for too long. Eventually the car will break down and malfunction. For others, their fight-or-flight system is underpowered and can't rev up at all, resulting in depression due to lack of energy and motivation.

In these situations, medications such as antidepressants can recalibrate the stress response system, repair any damage, and restore normal thinking or feeling. When thinking about the role of medication in your teen's recovery, here are some points to consider.[1]

DON'T RUSH TO MEDICATION

Sometimes our teens' anxiety or depression can be so bad that they need meds immediately. If they are having repeated panic attacks or not sleeping for nights in a row, or if they are harming themselves or thinking about it, then medication may be needed

---

1. Susan Amara, Raymond DePaulo, Philip W. Gold, and Carlos Zarate, "Can Depression Be Cured?," Library of Congress, May 5, 2016, http://stream.media.loc.gov/webcasts/captions/2016/160505klu1400.txt.

to provide urgent relief. However, apart from these emergency situations, before we turn to meds, we usually want to try the other means God has provided, many of which are explained in this book.

DON'T RULE OUT MEDICATION

None of us want our teens on meds, especially meds that influence thoughts and feelings. But we shouldn't rule them out in all circumstances. Sometimes our reluctance to even consider them is based on a misunderstanding of the connection between the fallenness of the body and our emotions. If our brain uses physical structures, chemistry, electricity, and so on to process our thoughts and emotions (and it does), then if any of that is broken, it's going to impact our thoughts and feelings.

DON'T WAIT TOO LONG

While rushing to meds is to be avoided, so is waiting too long. Let your family doctor be the best judge of when to introduce medications and which ones to try. Book a double appointment with your teen and tell the doctor as much as you can. Let him or her sort out what's relevant and what's not. Perhaps also let your teen speak alone with the doctor if that's what he or she wants.

DON'T RELY ON MEDICATION ALONE

Meds can be a vital part of a package of care, but rarely do they work if that's all we do. We need to use all the means that God has provided. Notice that this is only one chapter of many in this book. Try to take a holistic approach that addresses all areas of life.

DON'T EXPECT RAPID RESULTS

Some antianxiety drugs are very quick-acting and are suitable for emergencies. But these are not drugs we want anyone to be on long term. Other drugs, such as antidepressants, are safer in the longer term, and are also effective in treating anxiety, though they may take a few weeks to have a noticeable effect. There also may be some trial and error involved as the doctor determines which medication and dosage work best for your teen.

DON'T DWELL ON SIDE EFFECTS

A minority of people experience side effects from medications. Side effects should definitely be weighed, but so should the side effects of doing nothing. I've noticed that the people who think most about side effects are usually the people who experience them! Don't let your teen read the list as that will only increase anxiety levels. Just be on the lookout yourself for any changes.

DON'T STOP MEDICATION TOO RAPIDLY

One of the most common problems with these kinds of meds is that people come off them too quickly. They get impatient and give up. Or they begin to improve and then stop the medication before their bodies have fully recovered. Try to trust your doctor about when and how to come off your meds.

DON'T TELL EVERYONE

With almost every other medication, we get lots of sympathy and prayer support. Sadly, even in the church, there's still a lot of ignorance, prejudice, and misunderstanding around antianxiety and antidepressant medications. It's therefore often best not to tell others about your teen being on them. There will be some who understand, and you may confide in them. But we don't want to expose our teen to the kind of cruel bullying that can result if others find out they are taking meds for this.

PRAY FOR GOD'S BLESSING

If medications are God's gift, and I believe they are, then we want to ask for his blessing on them so that teens who need them get prescribed the right ones, that God will direct them to the parts of the body that need them most, and that they will work sooner rather than later so that our teens can eventually live without them.

TURNING THE KEY

1. *Engine illustration.* Use the analogy of revving up a car engine too much or too long to show how damage can occur through long-term stress. Also explain to your teen how every bodily system is damaged by sin and can be further damaged by trauma and other painful events. Just like someone's pancreas may be damaged, resulting in the need for insulin to control their sugar levels, so some people's fight-or-flight system is damaged and needs extra chemicals to restore it to normal.

2. *Family history.* You might want to explain the influence of genetics to your teen if anxiety or depression has played a part in your family history.

3. *Holistic.* Remember that just because there may be a physical component to depression or anxiety, that may not explain everything. It's important to explore what other factors are involved. For example, is there a background of abuse or bullying? Are there harmful patterns of thinking that need to be identified and changed? Is there sin that needs to be confessed and forsaken (guilt about pornography or other sexual desires and sins are common issues for teens)? Depending on the answers to these questions, your teen may need professional counseling and/or biblical counseling in addition to a doctor's help.

4. *Routine.* Meds work best when there is regularity in the rest of life. Work toward ensuring a regular daily routine of the same waking times, bedtimes, eating times, exercise times, and so on.

5. *Compliance.* Ensure compliance with taking medications. Depending on your kids, you may need to be in charge of administering the meds. It's very important that these are taken regularly every day, and to minimize side effects it's often best to take them in the evening before bed rather than in the morning.

6. *Positive.* Take a positive approach to meds, thanking God for them, praying together for his blessing on them, and encouraging teens that they will usually help and can speed up recovery.

6

FAITHLESS FLAVIA

Flavia was converted to Christ from a non-Christian back-ground. In her early Christian life, she found it easy to trust God for the salvation of her soul but struggled to trust him with the rest of her life. Her faith battled to believe that God was not only her Savior but also her protector and provider, especially when she saw lots of people dying in wars, natural disasters, school shootings, and so on. Having asked her pastor for help with her anxious unbelief, he started her on regular Bible reading and gave her some basic questions to guide her.

The Key of Scripture

The Bible is our foundation for addressing anxiety and depression in teens. Whether the cause is entirely spiritual, or whether it's a mix of spiritual, physical, mental, and relational factors, the Scriptures are basic and necessary to living a life of peace.

That's why we must get teens into the Bible. Obviously this is vital for teens that are not yet Christians, as it's the Scriptures that can make them wise unto salvation (2 Tim. 3:15). But even believing teens like Flavia need more knowledge of God to expel remaining unbelief and strengthen their faith. The Bible does this by bringing them into contact with the therapeutic power of the character of God, the promises of God, and the people of God. Here's how we can help our teens get into the Bible and benefit from biblical therapy.

READ THE BIBLE TOGETHER

While ideally our teens will be reading the Bible on their own, they may not be in that habit or they may have fallen out of that habit due to their anxiety or depression. That's why I'm suggesting that you make reading the Bible together a regular practice, at least to begin with. Some suitable passages to start with are:

- Exodus 14
- Psalm 23
- Psalm 27
- Psalm 42
- Psalm 46
- Psalm 56
- Psalm 73
- Psalm 139
- Isaiah 40
- Isaiah 41
- Matthew 6
- John 14
- Romans 8
- Philippians 4
- 2 Corinthians 1
- 2 Corinthians 12
- 1 Peter 5
- Hebrews 4

Be on the lookout for other passages in your own reading that you can use to encourage your teens.

Ideally you should have a set time each day when you read together. Perhaps you'll read just before they go to school or after supper or just before bed. If possible, read a few verses and then get them to read some verses, and so on. Keep it short. It's better to read a few verses that stick than overwhelm them with verses that just wash over them.

REMEMBER WHAT THE BIBLE IS

Every time you open the Bible, or talk about a Bible verse, remind your teen that we have the very word of God in our hands. Don't assume your child knows this or believes this. Instead, constantly remind them of the following two truths in particular.

God's word is reliable. The Bible is not just human opinion. As the very word of God, it is free of error and full of truth. It is totally dependable and should have the priority over all other human words, including the ones in our teens' minds.

God's word is powerful. God communicates his power through his word. These words are, therefore, the most powerful words in the world. The Bible is life-giving and life-healing.

ENCOURAGE INDEPENDENT READING

Once they are strong enough, you can suggest to your teens that they should also start reading the Bible on their own. Have them set aside a time for this each day, and start small. For maximum benefit, they should read their Bibles before they check their phones in the morning, and then again last thing at night. This will help them start their day and go to sleep with God's word uppermost in their minds. In their book I give specific suggestions for helping them get started in regular Bible reading.

WRITE OUT THE BIBLE

Your teen's anxiety or depression may be so severe that he or she can hardly concentrate. Focus can be fuzzy and distraction easy. That's why one of the exercises in every chapter of *Why Am I Feeling Like This?* is to write out verses suited to people with anxiety or depression. The very act of writing God's word helps to get it into teens' minds and hearts deeper than just reading it. They can also carry cards with verses written out on them in their pockets or stick them on the back of their phones so that they are reminded of God's truth throughout the day.

QUESTION THE BIBLE

As you read the Bible with your teen, keep the focus on the three areas highlighted by the following questions in *Why Am I Feeling Like This?*

- What does this teach us about God?
- What promise of God is in this passage?
- What do we learn about the people of God?

PRAY THE BIBLE

We'll look at this in more detail in a later chapter, but show your teen how to turn verses into prayers. For example, if reading about Christ's birth, praise God for the incarnation. When reading about a sin, confess it or pray against it. When reading about a Christian grace, ask God to give it to you and your loved ones, or to increase it. If you read about the ungodly, pray for the conversion of the ungodly. If you read about the church, pray for your own church. If you read about missions, pray for help to evangelize and witness as well as for God's blessing on missionaries you know. Using the Bible in this way will keep prayers fresh and biblical.

TALK ABOUT THE BIBLE

When teens are reading the Bible on their own, it's important to keep in spiritual contact with them. Maybe over supper or a cup of coffee, share what you read from the Bible that day and how it helped you, and ask them to do the same. The aim is to make talking about God's word as natural as possible and to model how to bring God's word into everyday life.

When anxiety is rising or your teens are getting overwhelmed, remind them of the verses you have read and learned together. Remind them of God's character, God's people, and God's promises. All of this should bring God's presence more and more into their lives and get them into the habit of recalling God's word even when you are not there to help them.

MEMORIZE THE BIBLE

As teens get mentally stronger, they can begin to memorize Scripture so that they can hide it in their hearts and minds and let it percolate through their lives even when they do not have a Bible in their hands. At the end of each chapter in their book, they'll find a verse to memorize.

TURNING THE KEY

1. *Model.* The most effective way to influence our teens in this area of Bible reading is to model it in our own lives. If our teens can see that the Bible is central and vital to our lives, they are much more likely to follow our example. Therefore:

- Read the Bible together as a family and as a married couple.
- Remind them how reliable and powerful the Bible is.
- Demonstrate independent personal Bible reading in your own life.
- Write out Bible verses on cards that you carry with you or stick on your phone.
- Question the Bible by asking the three simple questions: What does this teach us about God's character, promises, and people?
- Pray the Bible by connecting your prayers with what you read together.
- Talk about the Bible to your teen by sharing something from your reading each day.
- Memorize the Bible together by using the verses in the teen book.

2. *Checklist.* Read the ten-point checklist at the end of this chapter in the teen book and use it to guide and encourage your teen into the holy habit of daily Bible reading.

3. *Trust the instrument.* We don't want airline pilots who fly by their feelings. We want them to trust their instruments. Similarly, in the Christian life we don't want to live by our feelings but by the instrument God has provided—the Bible.

4. *The end.* The Bible is not the end but a means to an end, the end of getting to God and the peace this will bring (Isa. 26:3).

7

CONTROLLING COLIN

Colin suffered with obsessive-compulsive disorder (OCD), which was probably connected to the insecurity resulting from his dad leaving his mom and family when Colin was only three years old. He tried to stop his constant checking of locks and switches, but then he got agitated and angry. He hated any changes in his life because they made him feel as if things were out of control. His pastor's sermon on Philippians 4:6–7 ministered deeply to him as it directed him to replace his control with prayer to God.

The Key of Prayer

Philippians 4:6–7 are two of the most beautiful and encouraging verses in the whole Bible. They are especially helpful for the anxious, which was why we spent a whole chapter in the teen book unpacking these verses. I hope anxious teens will read this chapter and be encouraged to pray. How can we help our teens to practice these verses in their lives and therefore trust in God's control in all areas of life?

MEMORIZE TOGETHER

Why not join your teen in memorizing these verses together and challenging one another to repeat them without looking at the passage? Here are three tips for Scripture memorization so that you can help your teen with this exercise.

Divide the Verse into Small Chunks

Be anxious for nothing,
but in everything by prayer and supplication,
with thanksgiving,
let your requests be made known to God;
and the peace of God,
which surpasses all understanding,
will guard your hearts and minds through Christ Jesus.
(Phil. 4:6–7 NKJV)

Write Verses Out

Writing out verses can also help memorizing. You can write Scripture on an index card so that you can carry it with you and refer to it throughout the day.

Learn One Line at a Time

Read the first line out loud three times, then try to say it three times without looking at the verse. Once you've got one line solid in your memory, do the same with the next line. Read it out three times, then speak it three times without looking. Then try to say both the first and second lines together. Once you've got these solid, move on to the third line and so on.

Trying to do too much at once is like building a brick wall without mortar. You may make quick progress to begin with, but eventually it will all come tumbling down. Add mortar by taking it slowly, one line at a time, and don't add another until the mortar has set and the previous lines are secure in your mind. There are seven lines in this verse, so maybe take seven days to learn the entire thing, adding a line a day. Ideally you will do this at the same time each day, so that it becomes a habit you won't easily forget.

PRAY TOGETHER

It can be difficult for an anxious or depressed people to pray. They find it hard to get outside of themselves and to articulate their thoughts. They get so self-focused and confused that it can be challenging to focus on God and try to put sensible words together.

That's why it can be helpful to pray with your teen. Model the kind of prayer that's explained in the teen book. If you are memorizing the verses together, why not use that time to also pray with your teen and put this chapter into practice? Hopefully your teen will catch your example and begin to pray herself, but we can help her by having her follow us in prayer, praying our words after us until she gets the confidence to pray herself.

Remind your teens that God is listening. Show them how you take *everything* to God in prayer—the good things and the tough things. Also show them at different parts of the day how you stop to pray to God about various things and practice the culture of "everything and everywhere prayer." Be as specific as you can. Ask your teens what they want you to pray for.

Build a lot of thanksgiving into your prayers. This helps anxious teens who tend to focus on the negatives to see that God has actually blessed them with much already and gives a more balanced perspective on life.

PRAY APART

After some time of praying together and modeling Philippians 4:6–7 prayer, and after your teen has started to pray her own prayer after you, you then want her to engage in personal private prayer.

Discuss the best times and places where she can do this regularly and privately. Choosing the same time and place each day and/or each evening will help to build a habit that becomes more automatic. Tell your teen to just try a few minutes at a time.

Remind teens that God hears groans and cries and can make sense of them even when we can't. Encourage them to speak out the prayer rather than just saying it in their hearts. They can protect their privacy by whispering or by speaking quietly.

Ideally, they will gradually begin to pray throughout the day. Assure them that God is eager to hear them and that he keeps his promises. Perhaps after they have prayed, they can read Philippians 4:6–7 again and encourage themselves that God has heard them, he protects their hearts and minds, and he gives them peace, when they do this "through Christ Jesus."

This means that Jesus not only strengthens them to pray, but, through faith in him, Jesus presents their prayers perfectly to his Father in heaven and ensures they get a hearing and an answer. And when the peace of God begins to fill them and protect their hearts and minds, let's remember to turn our prayers and supplications into praise and worship. Even small improvements should be traced back to the God of peace who gives peace.

TURNING THE KEY

To help your teen begin to pray and benefit from prayer, keep the following words in mind.

1. *Honesty*. The psalmists do not hide their thoughts or feelings from God. They know God knows everything anyway, and therefore they pour out their hearts and minds before him. Bottling or covering things up helps no one. Model this for your teens by rejecting clichéd language and "Christian-speak" in your own prayers. Be transparent and open about where you are, and give your teen permission to do the same.

2. *Brevity*. Sometimes teens think they have to pray for ten to fifteen minutes to get God to hear them. But when they try that, they often fail and get discouraged. It's far better to pray for a minute or two at various points in the day. Help them associate prayer with meals or breaks and just shoot a few lines heavenward.

3. *Father*. Research has shown that what a person believes about God determines how much benefit a person gets from prayer. If we view God as distant and detached, there is much less personal benefit than if we believe him to be a loving heavenly Father who loves to hear and answer his children's prayers.

4. *Thanks*. Using prayer to remind ourselves of God's good gifts and thanking him for this is a therapy in itself. Get your teens to think of three things to thank God for in their home, in their friends, in their church, and at their school.

5. *Sovereignty*. Anxious teens like Colin attempt to overcome their anxiety by trying to control every tiny area of their lives. Although it's very hard, we must use these verses to help them hand over control of their lives to God. Depressed teens often feel like their lives are out of control. They too must be reminded of God's control. God's sovereign control is total and perfect and therefore trustworthy. Whether trying to control or feeling out of control, God's sovereignty is the remedy. Remind them continually, "God is in control." It takes humility to accept that and give control to God (1 Pet. 5:6).

6. *Turn right.* When you get on a plane, you don't turn left and get in the pilot's seat. You turn right and take a passenger's seat. When your kid is trying to control his life, remind him to "turn right."

7. *Reassurance.* We can't guarantee our teens that bad things won't happen, but we can reassure them that if they are believers, God will strengthen them to face any danger and that we will walk through it alongside them.

8

DEPRESSED DAN

Dan was shy and cautious by nature, but this mutated into disabling worry and fear in middle school. He was hypochondriacal about his health and never volunteered for anything out of fear he would mess up or get hurt. He had a tough home situation, with a violent alcoholic father and a mom who was preoccupied with caring for her elderly mother in their cramped house. School was no less stressful due to bullying, and therefore Dan spent most of his time at home locked in his bedroom playing video games. Sometimes he wished he were dead.

The Key of Elephant Training

Dan's situation seems hopeless. We look at his life and say, "No wonder he's depressed." Dan certainly deserves our sympathy for the painful events in his life that are not his fault. That's where we must start. But, however healing sympathy is, we must go further to really help Dan. We must challenge him to do some elephant training.

What do I mean by elephant training? I use the image of an elephant to illustrate the incredible power of our feelings in our lives. Like an elephant, if we let our emotions loose, they will go on the rampage and damage us and others. That's why we need to train our emotions, just as some people train elephants, so that they are kept under control and directed in a positive and helpful way. Psalm 77 gives us a good example of elephant training to follow when our teen's well-being is threatened by troubling events and feelings.

ADMIT THE TROUBLE

The psalms in general are very honest about the trouble that even good people experience in this life. They don't deny or minimize real difficulties. Show your teen that, although we don't know the details, Asaph the godly psalmist was also facing great trouble (Ps. 77:2). Bad things happen to good people. Just because bad things happen to our teens does not mean that they are bad people. Asaph teaches us that we shouldn't play down trouble, but face it and discuss it with one another and with God. Everyone goes through these times, and bad feelings are normal in such situations.

EXPRESS EMOTIONS

The next thing to highlight is that the psalms encourage the expression of feelings. Go through the first nine verses of Psalm 77, and ask your teen to identify the different emotions the psalmist is feeling and singing about. Look out for feelings of helplessness, depression, stress, anxiety, and so on. Although these are not happy or healthy feelings, Asaph did not squash them. He expressed them and, as God inspired him to sing about this in a psalm, it must be okay to do so.

God knows our teens' feelings anyway, so there's nothing to be gained by bottling them up and much to be gained by pouring out their hearts to the Lord. Tell them to tell God about their feelings. They will find considerable relief in this step alone. God wants to hear them express their feelings. Help them to learn emotional vocabulary and to articulate these feelings.

NOTICE THE CONNECTION

It's one thing to have bad things and bad feelings going on in our lives. It's another thing entirely to have bad thoughts about God. But that's where Asaph ends up because he not only expressed his emotions, but he let them dictate and distort his view of God and God's providence. Although he put it in question form, Asaph was wondering whether God was bad (Ps. 77:3), had abandoned him (v. 7), had changed (vv. 6–7), had broken his promises (v. 8), and had no mercy left (v. 9).

Do you see how Asaph's emotions were poisoning his thoughts about himself and God? His feelings were determining his theology. The elephant of his feelings was in control and winning! He felt these feelings and therefore thought these thoughts. It's important to help our teens make this connection between what they are feeling and what they are thinking, and the danger of letting feelings control their thoughts.

TAKE A TIME-OUT

How do we break this cycle of *Bad Trouble > Bad Feelings > Bad Thoughts*? How did Asaph do it in Psalm 77? The first thing he did was press pause. That's the meaning of *Selah* at the end of verse 9. It says "Stop, still, silence." Asaph recognized that his feelings were on the rampage, damaging his view of God, and he needed to stop this elephant before it did any more harm.

We need to help our teens do this when we see them stuck in this *Trouble > Feelings > Thoughts* cycle. Guide them to stop, be still, and be silent. Relaxation exercises can assist with this (see Tense Tom and Workaholic Will for more on this), so can exercise or a walk outside or praying with them.

In the calm and quiet, a sense of perspective begins to return. In Psalm 77:10 Asaph looks back on the first nine verses and says, "This is my *infirmity*" (KJV), meaning "weakness."[1] He realizes that he was weakening himself and his faith by letting his feelings control his thoughts. This is a pivotal point in the psalm and in Asaph's experience, because he doesn't just go back to his old habits; he starts a new habit.

---

1. Other versions translate verse 10 differently.

REORDER THE SEQUENCE

Instead of falling into the *Trouble > Feelings > Thoughts* sequence, he starts a new sequence of *Trouble > Thoughts > Feelings*. Asaph's trouble is still there—that hasn't changed. What has changed is his response to the trouble. God-centered biblical reasoning is now prioritized over feelings, resulting in much better and healthier emotions. In other words, there's a rider in the saddle that is controlling the elephant, so that his emotions are now under the direction of biblical thinking. This gives us hope that even though Dan's trouble is not going to be fixed any time soon, his response to it can improve.

FOCUS ON TRUTH

While Asaph's feelings were primary in verses 1–9, his thinking is first in verses 10–20. Notice all the "mind" verbs in verses 10–13: I will *remember*, I will *ponder*, I will *meditate*, and so on. That's what we need to direct our teens toward. Instead of "I feel" move them to "I will think," I will remember," and so on.

And what should our teens think about? The same as Asaph—God's character, God's word, God's works, God's people. Asaph fades into the background while God emerges in the foreground. We want Dan and others like him to realize that the way forward is not focusing on himself and his sad feelings but on God and his wonderful truth.

EXPERIENCE NEW FEELINGS

What happens to Asaph's feelings as a result of changing the sequence from *Trouble > Feelings > Thoughts* to *Trouble > Thoughts > Feelings*? What happens to the elephant of his emotions when it comes under the control of biblical reasoning? Interestingly, Asaph does not explicitly mention his feelings in verses 10–20 of Psalm 77. That's not because he now feels nothing. It's because his feelings are now secondary and his thoughts are primary. However, although his feelings are not explicit, we can still feel what he's feeling from the tone and content of verses 10–20. Read the psalm through and get a sense of how his emotional temperature has changed. We now sense confidence instead of doubt, optimism instead of pessimism, security instead of fear, comfort instead of distress, clarity instead of confusion, peace instead of anxiety, and joy instead of depression.

TURNING THE KEY

Bear these points in mind as you attempt to introduce elephant training to your teen.

1. *Be patient.* Although this psalm can be read in a couple of minutes, it doesn't mean that Asaph's feelings changed in a couple of minutes. Psalms like this are summaries of long battles. Likewise, with our teens, it can take a long time to change the default *Trouble > Feelings > Thoughts* sequence to the new *Trouble > Thoughts > Feelings* sequence.

2. *Be regular.* Because of the long-term nature of elephant training, it's important to set aside time each day or a few times a week to go through this with your teen. Schedule some times to sit down and talk about how your teen is feeling and thinking, and then work through the elephant training. It's best to do this frequently because the bigger the elephant grows, the harder it is to get it under control again.

3. *Be realistic.* In the teen book, Dan informed us that he was doing about 50 percent better after a couple of months of elephant training. That should be viewed as a success, especially given his ongoing family and school trials. We cannot expect teens with such troubles in their lives to be as peaceful or joyful as those without them.

4. *Be aware.* Due to hormonal changes there can be times when it's extremely difficult for teens to get their feelings under control. Their hormones are surging to levels they've never experienced before, creating powerful emotions, especially at certain times. Reasoning is weak against such feeling. This is especially true for girls with their monthly cycles. Be aware of this and adjust expectations accordingly.

9

NEGATIVE NICOLE

No matter how much went well in Nicole's life, she always focused on what went wrong. If there was a negative anywhere, she zoomed in on it to the exclusion of everything else. Even when she tried to enjoy hobbies, sports, or downtime, afterward she berated herself for wasting time that could have been spent on her studies.

The Key of Rethinking

While Dan's main problem had to do with his feelings, Nicole's is with her thinking. Instead of negative feelings dragging her down, negative thoughts are sinking her. Part of this is related to her upbringing. Her parents were incredibly demanding and criticized her severely if she did not ace everything she attempted. Over time, she adopted these voices as her own inner voice. This internal narrative resulted in default thinking patterns that distorted her view of herself and of reality, contributing to her emotional problems.

In the teen book, I highlight a number of false thinking patterns that may be contributing to teen anxiety and depression. We'll look at examples of these below because you will want to help your teens identify them when they are falling into them. But, although identifying them will make a difference, we have to go a step further and challenge them in order to change them.

The good news is that although repeated patterns of thinking and feeling create neurological connections and pathways that become a person's default way of thinking, they can be disconnected and rewired with practice. This is done primarily by asking questions, and the main one to ask with a view to transforming false thoughts is: "What fact or truth from God's world or God's word will help to change this thought and make it reflect reality better?"

Notice, first of all, that we must focus on what's true. This is not positive thinking that deceives us and our teens by thinking and believing things that are not true. We don't defeat a falsehood with another falsehood, but with the truth.

Second, there are two sources of truth. God's word is an obvious one, but there's also God's world. I'm referring to truth that is not found in the Bible, but rather in the world. For example, if someone says, "I'm useless at everything I try," we might look at her life and highlight a sport she's good at, friendships she has sustained, or a subject she does well in. These are not truths found in God's word but in God's world and can be used to bring a person to a more accurate assessment of themselves.

Third, this general question can be broken down into more specific questions depending on the false thinking pattern. Here are some examples to help you identify, challenge, and change your teen's false thoughts.

FALSE EXTREMES

Identify. Extreme thinking is the tendency to evaluate people and events as either a total failure or totally perfect. It is sometimes called all-or-nothing thinking because there is no in-between, no gray area. If one thing goes wrong for our teen, he might say, "I'm stupid," or "I'm worthless," or, "I'm a total failure."

Challenge: "Isn't there somewhere between perfection and failure? Yes, you made a mistake, but what also went right? What would be an accurate percentage score for this event or situation?"

FALSE GENERALIZATION

Identify: When one thing goes wrong, our teen generalizes that it will always be like this. "This always happens to me," or, "It's always going to be the same," or, "Nothing will ever go right." Look out for words like *always, none, never, no one, everyone,* and *all.*

Challenge: "Can you think of a time this went well? Why do you think that you will never succeed? Can you think of someone who got this wrong once but learned from it and went on to do well?"

FALSE FILTER

Identify. Our teen filters out the positive, and picks out the negative in every situation and thinks about it to the exclusion of everything else. He might get 95 percent in an exam but all he can think about is the missing 5 percent.

Challenge: "Why don't you take a look at the bigger picture? What are the positives here? You lost this friend, but how many friends do you have left? What about the 95 percent you got right?"

FALSE TRANSFORMATION

Identify. Our teen may transform neutral or positive experiences into negative ones. If she does well at something, she says, "I'll probably fail the next time." If someone compliments her, she says, "He doesn't mean it." If she does well, she says, "So-and-so did much better."

Challenge. "What's another way of looking at this? Why don't you try turning negatives into positives? What evidence do you have for saying that?"

FALSE MIND READING

Identify. Teens may think that they can tell what someone is thinking about them, that a person hates them or views them as stupid because he or she laughed at them.

Challenge. "Is it possible that he was laughing at something or someone else? How do you know that? How do you know what they were thinking about you? Is it possible to look at this another way?"

FALSE FORTUNE-TELLING

Identify. Sometimes teens make certain predictions such as "I will fail that exam and it will be a catastrophe." Or they ask lots of "what if" questions about the future: "What if I get anxious? What if I panic? What if . . ."

Challenge. "What's the likelihood/percentage chance of this happening? What's the worst consequence if it were to happen? If it does happen, is there a way of handling it?"

FALSE LENS

Identify. Mistakes are magnified and become catastrophes. "I injured my knee, and I'll never play sports again." Successes are minimized and belittled. "Everyone can do this. It's nothing special."

Challenge. "Why should such a mistake lead to such a catastrophe? Is there a way to make up for the mistake? Are there other possible outcomes that will not be so bad? Can everyone achieve this? What is special and unique about you?"

FALSE SHOULDS

Identify. Listen for a multiplying of unrealistic "shoulds" or "oughts." "I should do this . . . I ought to do that . . . I should be this . . . I ought to be able to do this . . ." In many cases these obligations are self-imposed and not in line with other people's expectations.

Challenge. "Who says you should? Why should you? How realistic is this? Who really expects that of themselves? How important is this, really?"

FALSE RESPONSIBILITY

Identify. This is when teens assume responsibility and blame themselves for a negative outcome, even when there is no basis for this. For example, when parents divorce, it's common for kids to blame themselves and feel responsible to bring their parents back together.

Challenge. "Who else is responsible for this situation? What percentage are you responsible for and what percentage are others responsible for?"

In this process, we are trying to substitute true and accurate thoughts for false and inaccurate thoughts. The way we do that is with truth. We present evidence that will help to argue against these thoughts, bringing our teens to more accurate conclusions and therefore more peaceful and joyful feelings.

TURNING THE KEY

1. *Courtroom illustration*. Read the teen's chapter and notice the way Nicole's counselor used the illustration of putting a falsehood on trial and then bringing witnesses and evidence to challenge the false thinking, find it guilty, condemn it to execution, and replace it with truth. Questions to ask your teen are:

- What false thought do you want to change? Another way to put this is "Write down a negative belief about yourself."
- What are the advantages and disadvantages of believing this false thought or belief?
- What is an alternative true thought or belief that you could think or believe?
- What are the advantages and disadvantages of believing this alternative thought?
- Compare the costs and benefits of both the false and the true belief. Which would you prefer to have?

2. *Practice*. Look for opportunities to practice this with your teen in a gentle and patient way. Teens may not get it initially, but eventually they will begin to understand and practice it on their own. Ideally you will do this for a brief time every day or so. It works even better if they keep a journal of times they got sad or anxious, writing down what they were thinking that made them feel like that.

3. *Highlight connections*. Highlight for your teen the connection between the negative thoughts and the negative feelings they are experiencing, but also the positive feelings that result from embracing positive truths about themselves.

10

WORKAHOLIC WILL

Like his dad, Will was a doer, always active, always working. He filled every day with busyness and then collapsed into bed for about five hours of sleep before rising to another day of constant motion. But eventually the years of chronic stress took a toll, and Will couldn't get his mind to slow down when he went to bed. He would lie awake for hours, his mind racing, his stomach churning. Unable to sleep at night and unable to sit during the day, he got more and more exhausted and stressed until even his dad got worried about him and took him to see a counselor at his church.

The Key of Rest

"Teens" and "rest" don't usually go together, do they? The teen years are busy years, restless years, hectic years. There's so much to do and so many opportunities that open up for sports, socializing, travel, work, and so on. However, such a restless nonstop lifestyle and culture is one of the main causes of the soaring anxiety levels among teens. The chronic stress and internal inflammation that result are extremely damaging to the bodies and minds of our teens.

One of the best things we can do for them, therefore, is to help them rest. This isn't going to be easy, but it's absolutely essential. This rest can be encouraged in three main areas: sleep, Sabbath, and relaxation. In the corresponding chapter of *Why Am I Feeling Like This?* I focus on the practical steps our teens can take in these areas. Here, I'd like to explain some of the science behind these practices in order to help you understand the connections between rest and health, and increase your motivation to direct and support your teens in these areas.

SLEEP

Although teens should ideally get about nine hours of sleep a night, most are getting only six to seven hours. Chronic sleep deprivation (less than six hours of sleep a night over a week) has serious physical, mental, emotional, moral, and spiritual consequences.[1]

For example, lack of sleep causes damaging changes to more than seven hundred genes. It even shows signs of causing brain tissue loss. It increases hunger, portion size, and preference for high-calorie, high-carb foods, with the resulting risk of obesity. It disrupts the brain's flow of epinephrine, dopamine, and serotonin, chemicals closely associated with mood and behavior. Thus, people with insomnia are ten times as likely to develop depression and seventeen times as likely to have significant anxiety. As Charlie Hoehn put it in *Play It Away,* "Eight hours of sleep is a miracle pill."[2] One of the reasons is that sleep flushes dangerous proteins from our brains, improving mental health, consolidating memories, and improving problem-solving abilities. That means the better we sleep, the better we learn.

No teen thrives spiritually when sleep-deprived. They are too tired to pray and read the Bible with any profit. Lack of sleep changes their outlook and makes them gloomy and pessimistic. Faith is harder, unbelief is easier, and willpower is weakened in the face of temptation.

In the teen book, I've given a number of tips for increasing the quantity and quality of sleep. Read them yourself and encourage your teens to implement these steps. If you do only one thing, ensure that their phone (and other digital technology) is removed

---

1. See chapter 3 in David Murray, *Reset: Living a Grace-Paced Life in a Burnout Culture* (Wheaton: Crossway, 2017).
2. Charlie Hoehn, *Play It Away: A Workaholic's Cure for Anxiety* (CharlieHoehn.com, February 7, 2014), 1081–1089, Kindle.

from their bedroom one hour before sleep time and charged overnight in the kitchen or living room.

SABBATH

I know there's a lot of disagreement about whether the Sabbath law still applies under the new covenant. Whether you believe this is an abiding law or not, I'm sure we can all agree on the divine benevolence behind the Sabbath principle and the corresponding human benefits. A lot of our resistance to establishing a weekly rest day is the result of viewing it entirely as a matter of law. Instead, I want you to think about it as a gift of God. That was Jesus's emphasis. The Sabbath was made for humanity, he insisted (Mark 2:27).

This was quite revolutionary in Jesus's day because the Pharisees had turned the Sabbath into a day of human performance that was given to God in expectation of a reward. Jesus said no, it's a day that God gives to humanity as a gift following six days of hard work. Jesus reframed it not so much as an obligation but as an opportunity.

It's a day where we can turn aside from all our work and rest with a good conscience. It's like God commanding that we eat chocolate to reduce our weight. Our response should be "Thank you!" rather than "No thanks!"

Try to reframe the Sabbath for yourselves and your teens as a gift of God, something he designed for our benefit in an unfallen world and that we need now more than ever in our fallen world. Viewed in that way, it's not something we *have* to do, but something we *get* to do.

Even secular corporations, institutions, and organizations like Sabbath Manifesto, are increasingly recognizing the benefits of a weekly rest day.[3] Science is finding more and more evidence of the physical, emotional, mental, and spiritual benefits that flow

---

3. See Sabbath Manifesto, http://www.sabbathmanifesto.org/. See also Emily McFarlan Miller, "The Science of Sabbath: How People Are Rediscovering Rest—and Claiming Its Benefits," Religion News Service, January 25, 2019, https://religionnews.com/2019/01/25/the-science-of-sabbath-how -people-are-rediscovering-rest-and-claiming-its-benefits/.

from this practice. Some general guidelines for starting this in your family are:

- Approach the Sabbath with joy and positivity.
- Center it around worship, going to church, learning about God, and fellowshiping with God's people.
- Don't overpack the day. It shouldn't be another hectic day of rushing from church activity to church activity.
- Make it a tech-free day. Give everyone's mind a break, even for part of it.
- Enjoy the creation, as God did on the first Sabbath. Feast your senses on all of God's works.

RELAXATION

In the corresponding chapter of the teen's book, I've given some guidance on breathing and relaxation techniques that relax the body and the mind. Don't worry: this can be done without ending up as a Buddhist! Perhaps find good books or YouTube videos that can guide you. I recommend that teens do these exercises first thing in the morning and last thing at night as well as times during the day when anxiety attacks or depression overwhelms. That way, we do both prevention and intervention. It's like showering every day but also using extra soap if we get especially dirty and sweaty from some activity.

Why not work alongside your teen in this? You could probably benefit from it too. Breathe together with him or her before panic attacks and when it attacks. If we want our teens to improve their mental and emotional health through improved sleep, receiving a weekly rest day, and practicing relaxation habits, we will need to practice this ourselves. It's not going to work if we ask them to do what we won't do. Our model will be far more influential than our words.

TURNING THE KEY

1. *Lifestyle example.* One of the biggest lessons from Will's story is that he copied his dad's pace of life. Will did this consciously, but many teens simply imbibe this unconsciously. Ask yourself how much your own lifestyle is contributing to your teen's problems. But also ask how a better example in these three areas of sleep, Sabbath, and relaxation can help your teen heal.

2. *Motivation.* Part of Will's counseling also explored the motivation behind his drivenness. Why did he feel the need to be so busy, so focused on success and performance? It's a question parents need to ask too. By exploring your own motives, you can help your teens identify theirs. If it is idolatry or human approval or some other sinful motive, then repentance and change is also required.

3. *Stress proof.* Read a book like Dr. Mithu Storoni's *Stress Proof* to find out about the damage we are doing to our brains with chronic stress. It will give you an X-ray of what we are doing to our most sensitive and precious organ and motivate you to steward it more carefully.

11

BEAUTIFUL BRIANNA

Brianna was obsessed with her appearance and what people thought of her. She spent all her money on new clothes and makeup, and she spent all her time on her image. Although the boys gave her a lot of attention, she was always fighting with her mom over her revealing clothes. Although the girls told her how pretty she was, she was insecure about her appearance. Although she could put on a smile, deep down she was very unhappy.

The Key of Identity

Do you sometimes look at your teen and ask, "Just who are you?"

Yesterday she had black hair; today she is blonde. Yesterday she was confident and cheerful; today she is morose and depressed. Yesterday she started a new fitness regime; today she is slobbing on the sofa. Yesterday she gave up Instagram forever; today she's been liking and posting for hours. Yesterday she talked with you for hours; today, she slammed her bedroom door on you and won't come out. You stare at the door and wonder, "Just who are you?"

One of the reasons for all this extreme and unpredictable behavior is that teens ask the same question about themselves: "Who am I?" It's a question few of us think about before our teen years. If you were to ask a five-year-old, "Who are you?" he would simply give his name. Push a bit further, and he might tell you who his parents are and where they live. That all changes in the teen and preteen years, as kids develop a sense of self, independent of their parents. They start choosing their own clothes, hairstyles, sports, pastimes, and friends. They are often more influenced by their peers than their parents, by popular culture than their home culture. They develop their own views on life, politics, society, religion, and so on. Soon, they are world experts on everything!

Some of this growing independence is normal; it's part of standard human development. But it's also a process that is corrupted by sin. Yes, it's to be expected that our kids will gradually pull away from us in the teen years as they become their own person. But there are many pitfalls in this process, and many ways this can go wrong and damage them.

TWO EXTREMES

Some parents overreact to this phase by trying to crush any independence or individuality in their children. But while this may work for a while, eventually kids will resent it and fight against it, often leading to outright rebellion and rejection.

Other parents can be too passive and abdicate any responsibility here. They let their kids be whatever they want to be. "We'll just let them decide how they want to identify." If their son identifies as girl, that's fine. If a daughter identifies as a lesbian, that's just the way she is. If she defines herself by the number of friends or likes on Instagram, no big deal. If athletic or academic success becomes her identity, we just let her pursue her dreams. If he wants to experiment with a different identity every day, we ignore it, even though he's getting more and more confused and stressed himself.

NAVIGATE TRANSITION

How then do we help our teens navigate this transition? How do we avoid the extremes of imposing our own identity on our children, or passively standing on the sidelines as their anxious confusion grows and their behavior becomes ever more bizarre?

First, recognize how influential this question is in their lives. Often when we are trying to change their sinful words or their behavior, the real problem is not what they are doing but who they think they are. If we want permanent change, we have to deal with the root, not the fruit. Try to figure out how they are answering the question "Who am I?" and how that is affecting them.

Second, talk to them about this question. Although there is a lot of talk about identity today, and some teens are aware of this issue in general, most do not understand how much their own identity issues are influencing themselves specifically. We can help our teens make more conscious choices in this area by talking to them about how they are answering this question, "Who am I?" We can also try to show how this question may be influencing others in their friend circle.

Third, help them see what they are allowing to shape their identity. Is it peers? Is it their past? Is it their successes or failures? Is it the media or social media? Is it grades or sports? Is it their body shape? Is it their sexual desires at that moment in time? Explain how many of these things are constantly changing throughout the teen years, others are out of their control, and others are simply distortions.

GOD-GIVEN IDENTITY

Finally, encourage them to seek a God-given identity. Instead of getting their identity from you, their friends, their culture, their success, their sexual desires, and so on, direct them to the God who created them and knows them better than we do or even they do. The simplest way to approach this subject is to think in terms of four steps.

Step One: I Am an Image Bearer of God

God has put his image on every single person (Gen. 1:27; James 3:9). This is true of everybody. That's what makes us human and separates us from animals. We are image bearers of God. That fundamental identity means that our teens' primary purpose in this world is to bear God's image, to show who he is, not who they are. They are to show God's mind, heart, and character in all that they are, say, and do. That means their first question should not be "Who am I?" but "Who is God?" Answering "Who is God?" first will then help divine image bearers to answer "Who am I?"

Step Two: I Am a Sinner

Our teens are sinners. They are not perfect human beings and never will be. Despite being called to be image bearers of God, their sin distorts and hides God's image from themselves and others. It's vital that they own sinfulness as part of their identity for two reasons. First, it creates a fundamental humility and distrust of themselves. As faulty and fallen, they must confess that their views of themselves and of others are liable to be skewed and wrong. Second, it releases them from impossible and depressing perfectionism. Admitting their sins and mistakes to God and seeking his forgiveness as a normal part of life can be relieving and liberating.

Step Three: I Am a Christian

If our teens are to overcome their sin and fulfill their calling to bear God's image in the world, they must be born again and converted to Christ. When that happens, "I am a Christian" becomes the core of their identity. As such, they become "Christ-bearers," they bear the image of Christ, who is the perfect image of God (Heb. 1:3). In a way, becoming a Christian begins the removal of their sinfulness and the restoration of the image of God. It's getting us back to who we were created to be. The more our converted teens can grasp the enormity of their new identity as Christians, as Christ-bearers, the healthier and happier they will be. That's why, in the teen book, I've listed some of the multiple ways Christian identity is presented in the Bible. In some ways, God's message to the Christian is "Become who you are" (Rom. 6:11).

Until our teens are Christians, identity issues are going to be difficult to overcome. While enduring stability of identity is unlikely until they are converted to Christ, step four is also relevant to unbelieving teens.

Step Four: I Am Unique

Although steps one through three are true of all Christian teens, step four differentiates them as distinct, special, and unique human beings. Our teens go wrong when they make their uniqueness the most important part of their identity. But they and we can also go wrong if we do not recognize that God has made each of his image bearers different. God does not create clones, and parents shouldn't try to either. God has given each of his image bearers a unique personality and character, with unique gifts and callings. Our teens are therefore to ask him, "Who do you want me to be?" and "What do you want me to do?"

TURNING THE KEY

1. *Personal identity.* Use this chapter to work through your own identity issues. You will understand your teen better if you understand yourself better. Walk through the four steps and consider how much your identity shapes your words, clothing, actions, relationships, and so on.

2. *Four steps.* As parents, one of the most loving things we can do for our children is help them discover their God-given identity by constantly walking them through these four steps. When they do this, it will work much good at the root of their beings, killing bad fruit and producing good.

3. *Who am I?* If your teen is willing, have her write down all the words that come to mind when she answers the "Who am I?" question (e.g., student, athlete, failure, bad, lonely). Then work through the description with these questions:

- What is true and to be changed?
- What is true and not to be changed?
- What is true and not included?
- What is false and to be changed?

12

MEDIA MAX

Max was so addicted to digital technology that he was beginning to fear it was damaging his brain. He also noticed that he got angsty and depressed after playing online games for hours. Max's worst fears were confirmed when a speaker at his youth group presented the latest science about how overexposure to digital technology is changing our brains, our bodies, and our feelings—for the worse. He was also convicted about his porn habit.

The Key of Digital Detox

All the research on the epidemic of teen anxiety and depression lays the greatest blame upon the overuse and misuse of digital technology. Why is this so dangerous for our teens' mental and emotional health? First, there's the constant hyperstimulation and neurological agitation, with the brain never getting downtime and a chance to rest. Then, there's the addictive element built into the technology by device manufacturers and software companies. Late-night technology use is also the major culprit in the drastic sleep deprivation among teens, which damages the body and mind. The "compare and despair" aspect of social media and the guilt and bondage of online porn are also significant factors in teen anxiety and depression.

Put it all together and you have a well-oiled depression and anxiety machine. Basically, our teens will never recover from anxiety and depression until they get digital technology under control. No matter what else you do, if you don't deal with this, all your other efforts will be in vain. If you doubt me, read Dr. Jean Twenge's book, *iGen: Why Today's Super-Connected Kids Are Growing Up Less Rebellious, More Tolerant, Less Happy—and Completely Unprepared for Adulthood—and What That Means for the Rest of Us*. So how do we help our kids with this massive challenge?

NO TECHNOLOGY

Some parents are probably still trying the "no technology" approach.[1] They say, "The dangers are too great; the consequences are too awful. Therefore, separate from the world by rejecting technology. We won't buy it, and we'll ban our children from using it, too."

This approach is admirable and understandable, but impossible. Digital technology is so pervasive that trying to avoid it is like trying to avoid breathing. Our children will find it, or it will find them. They will then be using it without our knowledge and without any training and teaching—probably the worst of all worlds.

Having said that, sometimes we have reason to remove all digital technology for a limited season in order to give the brain time to recover from the damage done by overuse of technology. Dr. Victoria Dunckley's book, *Reset Your Child's Brain: A Four-Week Plan to End Meltdowns, Raise Grades, and Boost Social Skills by Reversing the Effects of Electronic Screen-Time*, explains the why and the how of this.

MORE TECHNOLOGY

Other people try the "more technology" strategy, the idea being that we use good technology to defeat bad technology. We set up passwords and time limits on home computers; we add tracking apps to our children's cell phones; we install accountability software on laptops, and so on.

---

1. This material on the challenges of technology first appeared in my article "Digital Detox" in *Tabletalk Magazine*, October 1, 2016.

All of these things are good and can certainly be helpful parts of an overall package of caring for ourselves and our children.[2] But we must remember that we can never get enough good technology to beat bad technology. Teens are especially adept at circumventing controls and finding loopholes in the most secure systems. They can always find more technology to beat our "more technology" battle plan. They can always find another device and hide it from us.

We need more than "more technology." We, and our teens, need more theology and more relationship. We can take practical steps too, which I've outlined in the teen's chapter on this subject. However, the practical must be built on a foundation of more theology and more relationship, and that's where you come in as parents.

MORE THEOLOGY

If we want a deep, lasting, and spiritual solution, we need to teach our kids deep, lasting, and spiritual truths. Strong digital theology is the answer to damaging digital technology; the oldest truths are the best rebuttal to the newest challenges. More Trinity is more effective than more technology. Here's a sample of truths to teach our teens as the foundation of using technology for God's glory instead of personal harm.

God is all-knowing. While they may escape our eyes and get around accountability software, teens cannot escape God's eye or get around his accountability. He sees every place, every second, every screen, every click, every tap. He has a daily report of all the sites visited, all the messages sent, and all the pictures viewed. If we really knew that he knows, what a difference that would make.

God is Judge. God will one day call everyone to account not just for every idle word but for every idle click, for every second spent in pointless time-wasting, for every abuse of self and others. No one can escape the judgment of God. May his impending final

2. Tim Challies, "The Porn-Free Family Plan," Challies.com, April 15, 2014, https://www.challies.com/articles/the-porn-free-family-plan/. See also the Freedom app, www.freedom.to/ and Covenant Eyes, www.covenanteyes.com.

judgment compel our teens to make better daily judgments in their use of technology.

God is Savior. Sometimes a sense of guilt stops sin. More often, guilt multiplies sin. It leaves our kids hopeless and despairing. They think, "I've sinned yet again with my cell phone. I'm condemned. What's the point in trying anymore?" Guilt also multiplies sin by creating distance between them and God. That's why they need to hear about salvation, grace, and forgiveness all over again. Nothing deters sin like the forgiveness of sin because it not only removes guilt, it also multiplies love for the forgiver (Luke 7:47). This is especially important to communicate if our teen has been using porn.

God is powerful. We need to remind our kids, especially when they feel helpless before the powerful forces of technology, that God is greater, far greater. With God, all things are possible, and he loves to demonstrate his possibility—especially in our impossibility. He can give our children the Holy Spirit to resist temptation and enable them to do what is right and good. His Spirit is far more influential than the spirit of the age.

God is in the quiet. As Elijah discovered, God's voice is often found in quiet. That's why the psalmist said, "Be still, and know that I am God" (Ps. 46:10). If our teens want to hear God's voice, they must make stillness and silence a priority. In general, the more they are connected to their phones, the more they are disconnected from God.

MORE RELATIONSHIP

Whatever the state of our present relationship with our teens, we must prayerfully prioritize connection and conversation with them. Deeper relationships are more effective than more detailed rules. So, we've got to work at opening and maintaining the channels of communication. Rules always work better within the context of relationship. Discuss the positives of technology and use it to share good things with them. Don't make the only element of your relationship their misuse of technology. Try to find time to talk about their thoughts, feelings, and opinions about various things. Conversation should not always be focused on schedule, commitments, and schoolwork.

TURNING THE KEY

1. *Educate.* I've already mentioned a couple of books to persuade you of the dangers of technology. If you are already convinced and now want practical advice on how to get digital technology under control, the best book is Andy Crouch's *The Tech-Wise Family: Everyday Steps for Putting Technology in Its Proper Place.* It's a realistic yet challenging book with a game plan for families to put technology in its place. See his list of Ten Commitments that every family can work toward.

2. *Delay.* Don't be an early adopter or giver of technology. The later we can introduce our kids to technology, the better. In general, the more maturity they have, the safer they will be.

3. *Prepare.* The worst thing in the world we can do is throw our kids a phone and walk away. We might as well drop them in the Amazon without any protection. We've got to prepare them for the digital jungle by explaining the dangers they will face and what to do when they meet them. Some of our kids will be more vulnerable than others.

4. *Gradual.* Rather than let them access everything right away, you can use parental controls to limit the number and kind of apps they can access. Start with texting, for example, then add email, then some specified websites, and so on. Limit also the time on their devices, gradually increasing it, but rarely should their total daily time be over an hour. Ideally it should be closer to thirty minutes.

5. *Monitor.* You have a right and duty to monitor your kids' use of digital technology. This can be done in various ways at the device level using Covenant Eyes, and also at the home level using router technology such as Circle. Be especially on the lookout for cyberbullying. (See Tim Challies's porn-free family plan at www.challies.com/articles/the-porn-free-family-plan/.)

6. *Review.* Go over your kids' technology use every couple of weeks. Ask them how it's going and if they have any questions. Share any concerns that you have with their technology use. Reward good use with more access and sanction misuse with limitations. If they confess misuse, then sanctions should be lightened.

7. *Discern.* The aim is to help our teens increase in digital discernment, in understanding what is helpful to them and what is harmful. Talk through good examples of their social media posts and also discuss the bad or unwise ones. Talk to them about the impact of dwelling on negative news stories and images. Discuss the importance of developing real-life relationships more than a digital identity.

8. *Model.* If we can't control digital technology, then neither will they. Do we text while driving or at the supper table? So will they. Do we use our devices last thing at night? So will they. Do we resist accountability? Then so will they. Why not join them in filling out the digital detox questionnaire at www.whyamIfeelinglikethis.com /digitaldetox.

9. *Confess.* If you have failed to parent your teen well in this area, then confess to God, and then to your child, and ask for forgiveness before trying to reverse the damage and change the practices.

10. *Pray.* Our children are born with depraved hearts. They will therefore love darkness rather than light. They are going to be attracted to the dark side of the internet. So we must pray for them to be born again. Pray that God would replace a love of darkness with a love for the light. We can train, legislate, and hover, but above all we must pray that our children would ultimately live and obey not out of fear of the law but out of love for Christ.[3]

3. This step first appeared in my article "7 Steps for Using Technology for God's Glory," Christianity.com, January 4, 2013, https://www.christianity.com/christian-life/discipleship/7-steps-to -using-technology-for-god-s-glory.html.

13

FRIENDLY FIONA

Fiona's life revolved around friends—getting them, keeping them, and pleasing them. Her stress over this multiplied when she started a relationship with an older boy. Although her friends thought he was amazing, he quickly made clear that he wanted a sexual relationship with her. He pressured her to send nudes, which she did. But he shared them with his friends, and she can't face going to school now because everyone is either laughing at her or calling her names. Some days she feels suicidal.

The Key of Christ's Friendship

Relationships play a massive role in our teens' emotional and mental health, both for good and for harm. We therefore want to teach them how to cultivate healthy relationships and manage or resolve difficult ones. That's why the next few chapters are about making and managing relationships with friends, with enemies, and with parents.

In the corresponding chapter of *Why Am I Feeling Like This?* I cover friendship in general, with a few specific remarks about friendships with the opposite sex. Here, I will deal briefly with friendships in general, and then focus on boyfriend/girlfriend relationships so that you can guide teens through this maze. I'm going to address parents of teen girls especially, partly because it's too awkward to keep referring to both sexes, but also because girls tend to suffer more pain in this area than boys. But much of what I say applies to parents of boys too, so just make the switch as you read.

THE WORSHIP OF FRIENDS

The main point is not to turn friends into a god. That can happen by investing too much in one friend or by measuring oneself by the number of friends one has. If teens invest too much in one friend, then they will always be anxious about losing that friend. If they have too many friends, there will be too much drama as it's impossible for teens to successfully manage multiple relationships. There will always be drama going on somewhere. Ideally, our kids will have a circle of three to four friends, not too many to manage, not so few that the loss of one becomes the loss of everything.

Encourage your kids to follow Jesus in viewing friendships primarily as an opportunity to serve and help others, rather than a source of satisfaction or status. That approach will also reduce possessiveness by seeing the sharing of a friend with others as a positive.

THE IMPORTANCE OF DADS

Girls will often confide more in their moms about relationship issues. However, it's vital for dads to be involved in their teen daughters' lives. Although girls may not talk to their dads about relationships, it's important for dads to spend time with their daughters, encourage their daughters, praise their daughters, hug their daughters, and appreciate their daughters. Sometimes girls who lack such a father figure may seek out an alternative form of male affirmation in older boys. Girls who have strong and secure relationships with their fathers are less likely to do this.

If, for whatever reason, your daughter's father is absent from her life or cannot be depended upon for this kind of relationship, then perhaps you and she can find trusted father figures from your church or extended family. However, even if that's not possible, our heavenly Father is more than able to fulfill this role in your daughter's life, and you can constantly encourage her to look to him.

THE WISDOM OF DELAY

In popular culture, kids are encouraged to be in romantic relationships at younger and younger ages. It's happening as early as elementary school. Ideally, we want to delay romantic relationships until after high school. That's the rule we started with as a family, and the one time we made an exception, we soon regretted it.

The fact is that 90 percent of high school romances do not last beyond three months. They almost always end in painful heartbreak, especially for girls, leaving lingering emotional scars. Our teens just don't have the emotional maturity for such relationships at this stage in their lives. Even if a relationship does last longer than three months, there's so much uncertainty and drama in the ups and downs that it's a major stressor and also a distractor from studies.

Teen boys have no idea about the emotional pain they inflict upon girls by the way they relate to them. They are also under pressure from their hormones and their peers to sexualize the relationship as soon as possible, often resulting in them forcing girls to do things they do not want to do, and then exposing them to ridicule when they break up by spreading pictures or stories.

THE VALUE OF GROUPS

It is far better to get to know the opposite sex in group settings than one-on-one. As your teens get older, encourage them to include boys in their social gatherings so that they can get used to what boys are like—how they act and communicate—without the complication of romance. Three things always to check in these settings are that a responsible parent is in the vicinity to supervise, that no alcohol or drugs are being consumed, and that they are coming home with a responsible driver at a reasonable hour. Even though group settings are safer than one-on-ones, we are still responsible to protect our children there, and therefore we should find out the names and characters of those who will be there.

THE PRIORITY OF JESUS

In the teen book, I put Jesus at the center of friendship because this is the most important friendship and it influences all the others. One of the best things we can do for our teens is to help them put and keep Jesus at the center of their lives and make him their number one friend. If this is their foundation, then their lives will have stability, regardless of what is happening in their other relationships.

It will also mean that when they are ready to pursue romance, they will prioritize finding someone who also loves Jesus and wants to honor and serve him.

When a young couple begin a closer relationship, my main advice is to make spiritual conversation a major part of the relationship. They should be talking to one another about their faith and what they are reading in the Bible, praying together about their relationship, and maybe reading Christian books or listening to sermons together. With that in place, they are in a safer place to eventually, slowly, and gradually increase physical contact to appropriate and agreed-upon levels. I've given some general guidance on this in the teen book, but I'd encourage you to keep this conversation going with them throughout any relationship.

THE WELCOME OF GRACE

Whatever happens in our kids' relationships with others, as parents we must be there for them no matter what. If they mess up, if they sin, if they have broken hearts, we must care for them, show them grace, point them to Jesus, and assure them that our love for them will never change. Share your own disasters and pains. Encourage them that in Jesus there is grace for sinners and healing for the broken. Pray with them that God would not only take away guilt and heal their hearts but give them wisdom about future relationships.

TURNING THE KEY

1. *Preemptive conversation.* In the last chapter, I talked about the importance of starting a conversation with our kids about digital technology before it becomes a problem. The same goes for friendships. It's best to establish good biblical and common-sense principles before problems arise. Start this discussion at an early age and adjust rules and advice as they get older and prove themselves to you.

2. *Jesus's friendship.* Show your kids how Jesus is the best friend we could have and what a difference his friendship makes to how you view and handle all other friendships.

3. *Pray for your kids' friends.* Pray that God would give your children good friends and that these friends would be blessed and be a blessing in this friendship. Pray with your kids about this and pray with them for a future friendship with someone who will become their husband or wife.

4. *Keep talking.* Always be available to talk through friendship issues. Assure teens that you want to know about their lives, that problems are common, and that having friendship difficulties doesn't make them weird. Girls are more likely to want and take the opportunity to talk than boys.

14

BULLIED BENTON

Benton was the victim of school bullies. It started with verbal assaults, but progressed to physical threats and pushes. He tried to avoid them at school, but when that didn't work, he started skipping classes. When his grades started falling, his parents and guidance counselor expressed concern, but Benton was too afraid to tell them. To make matters worse, his tormentors got his cell number and started bullying him at home via messages and pictures. He's now having night-mares and panic attacks.

The Key of Protection

One of the most painful experiences of a parent is watching their child endure bullying, especially because we see the fear and anxiety that always accompanies it. It can get so bad that teens may think about ending their own lives or even actually attempt suicide. How do we parent in such serious circumstances?

RECOGNIZE BULLYING

The most basic form of bullying is physical, and is more common among boys than girls. However, verbal, nonverbal, and cyberbullying are far more common today, especially among girls. Verbal bullying is when one or more teens combine threats, insults, mocking, and lies to traumatize another person with fear and shame. Nonverbal bullying is when one or more teens shun another teen, shutting him or her out from friend circles, sports, social occasions, and so on. Cyberbullying is when teens use digital media to attack or undermine another teen.

While physical, verbal, and nonverbal bullying have always been with us, online bullying has only been with us for ten years or so and has played a large part in the rise of teen anxiety in recent years. It is much harder to discover, identify, and deal with because it usually happens through our teens' phones, there are no other witnesses to it, and removing our teen from school or other places does not stop the harassment. It used to be that when teens were home, they were safe, but now bullies have access to them 24/7. Screen use has also had the effect of reducing the levels of empathy in kids, making bullying easier.

PREPARE FOR BULLYING

Bullying is part of sinful human nature, I'm afraid. We're not going to eliminate it. As almost every kid goes through it to some degree or other at some point or other, we need to prepare our kids for it.

Bullying varies. Teach them about the different kinds of bullying so they know what to look out for and can recognize it when they see it or experience it.

Bullying is wicked. Emphasize how wicked bullying is, how offensive to God and damaging to others, so that they never engage in it themselves and they don't blame themselves if it happens to them.

Bullying can be provoked. As some teens through their words or actions may aggravate others, show them how to be wise in their words and actions so that they don't provoke bullies.

Bullying can be reduced. Because bullies often pick on those who look different or weak, two ways to reduce bullying are to minimize differences in physical appearance and to project confidence in posture, expression, and walk. Give your kids resources about bullying before it takes place to reduce the likelihood of it happening.

Don't wait for them to come to you, but regularly ask them if they are experiencing any kind of bullying, and encourage them to show you any online harassment they may be experiencing. Assure them you care. Get in the habit of asking them about their school day and looking out for any significant changes in them.

RESPOND TO BULLYING

So what do you do if you discover your teen is being bullied? This partly depends on the severity of the situation, so I'll suggest a number of phases that gradually increase in seriousness. You will need to pray for wisdom in decisions about which phase to start with and how quickly to go through them. The ideal is for the early phases to work so that the more serious actions will not be required.

Phase One: Patient Support

I'm afraid that some degree of bullying is simply a fact of life. We can't protect our kids from every challenge or unpleasant experience, and it wouldn't be good for them either. They're going to get hard knocks as they grow up; they're going to experience various kinds of bullying in college, in the workplace, and in many other spheres. Part of parenting is helping our kids endure and persevere through low-level bullying. I do not include any bullying in this category that injures a child or threatens his or her life.

In this phase, we want to listen to our kids' experiences, show them that we understand and sympathize, perhaps offer some guidance as to what to say and do when it happens, pray with them, and encourage them to keep us informed. Brainstorm with them, encouraging them to come up with solutions and talking them through. Maybe practice some of these with your child in role-play.

Let teens know that this is common, that you went through it, as do most people, and that it will ultimately make them stronger. Low-level bullying will often fade away of its own accord, especially if your teen does not retaliate.

If it's online bullying, perhaps help your teen to block the bully or change the phone number or delete certain apps, at least for a time. Bullies will often give up if they know they are not getting through to their targets.

Phase Two: Skilled Intervention

If the low-level bullying persists too long or if the bullying is more serious, then some kind of intervention is required.

It rarely helps the situation for a parent to address a bully directly, and therefore we want to usually involve a mediator that has some level of skill with these situations. Most schools today have trained and experienced personnel that can offer advice or intervene in ways that will maximize the chances of success. A pastor or coach may also be approached if it's taking place in church or in sporting activities.

It can help if you emphasize that, at this point, you don't want the bully punished; you just want the bullying stopped. Also, you should say that if your child has in any way contributed to this, you want to know about it. This shows that you have not determined to be one-sided. It might help to have some evidence of the bullying such as cuts or bruises or screenshots of messages.

The ideal is that teachers, pastors, and other adults who have been informed about the problem will be on the lookout for bullying and will intervene based on what they see rather than what has been reported to them. Increased adult supervision at certain times and places may be appropriate. It is also helpful when older respected teens take bullied teens under their wings and show others they are not alone.

Phase Three: Pursue Justice

Hopefully we won't need to move to phase three, but depending on the nature of the bullying, the effect upon your teen, and the success or otherwise of mediation, you may need to eventually file a complaint with the authorities God has appointed to punish evildoers and protect the innocent, whether that is the school or the police (Rom. 13:1–4). This is obviously a very serious step and may require temporary or permanent removal of your teen from school to prevent possible reprisals.

THE WORST-EVER BULLYING

Throughout all of this, remind your teen that although Jesus was the least deserving of bullying, he endured the worst-ever bullying at the hands of the worst-ever bullies. He therefore not only models how to respond to this (1 Pet. 2:20–25), but can understand and sympathize with what they are going through. Encourage your teens to talk to Jesus about what they are experiencing and remind them that Jesus endured this to save sinners from their sin.

TURNING THE KEY

1. *Watch*. Look out for signs of bullying. These include marks on the body, damaged clothes or property, not wanting to go to school, withdrawal from social contact, or fear when our teens get a notification on their phone.

2. *Ask*. It's good to ask our kids regularly about whether they are getting bullied, but definitely do so if you suspect they are being bullied. Assure them that you're not going to visit anyone's house or call anyone's parents.

3. *Pray*. Pray with your teen about the bullying. Pray for his or her protection, for patience, for courage, and for wisdom on how to handle it. Pray for the bully or bullies.

4. *Teach*. Guide your teens in how to avoid situations or how to get out of them when they are in them. You can find many good guides online.

5. *Involve*. Find out from your school which adults are responsible for handling bullying. Usually someone on the staff has had specialized training and knows how to intervene with maximum chance of success.

6. *Medication*. If bullying has been violent or has been going on too long, then mild PTSD is possible, and that may require medication to return the overactive fight-or-flight system to normal.

15

REBELLIOUS ROB

Rob resented how strict his parents were compared with other parents. His resentment frequently boiled over in angry outbursts and arguments. This resulted in various forms of discipline, which only made Rob even more rebellious. Filled with hate and anger, he started sliding into depression. His concerned parents want him to see a counselor but he thinks it's they that need the counselor.

The Key of Respect

Much teen anxiety stems from serious or sustained conflict with their parents. This causes chronic stress and inflammation of their bodily systems with many harmful consequences. We therefore need to understand this area and think of ways to minimize such conflict.

A CHANGING RELATIONSHIP

While raising children inevitably produces conflicts from time to time, we need to recognize that disagreements are probably going to increase exponentially in the teen years. Our children are growing into young adults, taking on more responsibility, enjoying more freedom, and being exposed to more outside influences. They are thinking more independently and beginning to assert their own wills and make their own choices. They have transportation that allows them increased mobility and work opportunities.

All these changes can produce disagreement and conflict unless we change and adapt our relationship with our teens. If we treat our kids like ten-year-olds when they are fifteen, we are going to produce a lot of unnecessary conflict.

A POSITIVE RELATIONSHIP

It's important to maintain a positive relationship with our teens. Sometimes we end up with a relationship that involves only correction and criticism. This will inevitably distance us from them and make our attempts at correction ineffective.

Correction has to be in the context of positive activities and interactions if we are to have any hope of success. We therefore want to make a point of talking to our teens about their lives, every part of them. Take them out for breakfast, take them camping, go fishing, play ball, meet for coffee, go on trips and vacations together. Show your interest in their sports and hobbies by attending and funding them. Build up a reserve of positivity, otherwise correction will result in relational bankruptcy.

A LISTENING RELATIONSHIP

When our kids are seven and eight, we give their immature opinions and views limited attention. However, as our teens get older, they actually can begin to make sense. We need to learn how to listen to them and not dismiss them. Listen to them when they bring concerns to you or as they respond to your rebukes. Even if they do it wrongly, there may be some truth in what they say. Sometimes it may be appropriate to pause in our responses and ask for time to think about what they have said to us. If they can get a sense that we are listening and thinking about what they say, it can take a lot of heat out of the situation.

A PEACEMAKING RELATIONSHIP

As conflict is inevitable, we must learn how to be a peacemaker like Jesus. In *Why Am I Feeling Like This?* I've tried to teach our teens how to do this from their side of things, but we parents must also learn our part in this. You can find practical direction on this in the Turning the Key section below. Remember that we are training our teens for future conflicts they will face among friends, at school, at work, and in their own future homes. They will approach disagreements much as they have seen at home. Sometimes a pastor or a counselor that specializes in family issues can be a helpful mediator in serious parent-child disputes. They can bring a measure of objectivity as well as lower the emotional temperature.

A DISCIPLINED RELATIONSHIP

If our teens disobey or disrespect us, we may need to impose disciplinary sanctions. Through the apostle Paul, God gave fathers the primary responsibility for disciplining their children, but he also warned fathers about the danger of provoking their children to anger (Eph. 6:4). If you want to exasperate your children, here are ten ways to do it:

- *Excessive discipline* is too frequent or too hard.
- *Disproportionate discipline* is way out of scale to the offense.
- *Inconsistent discipline* punishes for an offense one day but not on most other days.
- *Prejudiced discipline* unfairly favors one child over another.
- *Humiliating discipline* aims to belittle and shame.
- *Public discipline* makes no attempt to hide the child's offenses and punishment from others.
- *Bad-tempered discipline* is terrifyingly out of control.
- *Prayerless discipline* practices no prayer before, during, or after the discipline.
- *Heartless discipline* makes no attempt to get behind the why of the wrong and show the child the need for heart-change.
- *Selfish discipline* takes frustrations out on the child to make the parent feel better.

Do the opposite if you want to discipline in a way that does not add to your teen's anxiety.

A PATIENT RELATIONSHIP

Although we want instant results from our teaching and our discipline, usually the fruit takes some years to show even a little green shoot (Heb. 12:11). In the meantime, impatience, anger, and bad temper can destroy relationships and communication. We might modify our teens' behavior for a time, but we lose their hearts.

Let's try to remember how patient God has been with us as he has parented us, how slow to anger, how long-suffering, how plenteous in mercy he is. Let's remember that we are trying to show the character of our heavenly Father in our family.

Be especially patient in this whole area of anxiety and depression. God may have allowed this in your teen's life to teach you, or to strengthen your relationship with your teen. Work together using both the parents' guide and the teens' guide, and watch how God uses your teen's anxiety and depression for your spiritual good as well.

TURNING THE KEY

Learning from my own mistakes in parenting five kids (now ages six to twenty-three), here's what I advise to maximize the hopes of peacemaking even in the midst of conflict.

- *Don't pick on everything.* You have to pick your targets by prioritizing the most important issues. Some faults have to be overlooked, at least temporarily (Prov. 19:11).
- *Don't bottle anger up.* That's bad for you, and it's bad for your relationship. Pick a time when neither you nor your teens will be stressed and rushed, and try to speak firmly but lovingly.
- *Don't attack their person.* Say "you lied to me" rather than "you are a liar."
- *Don't speak generally.* Identify the specific fault and don't exaggerate. Keep the focus on the specific issue in question, and don't bring other faults up at this moment.
- *Don't base discipline on opinion.* If at all possible, show why your rules and sanctions are based on God's word rather than just your own opinion.
- *Don't make discipline about you.* Remind your kids that it is God, not you, that our kids have primarily offended, and that discipline is a duty God requires of parents rather than something you necessarily want to do.
- *Don't be one-sided.* Confess your own faults if necessary, and seek forgiveness even when there is more wrong on the other side.
- *Don't let the sun go down on your wrath (Eph. 4:26).* Forgive and forget. Don't bear grudges or keep resentments bubbling.
- *Don't limit communication to discipline.* Invest time in your kids' lives to build up relational capital with them.
- *Don't forget the gospel.* Give hope by explaining the way to forgiveness through repentance and faith in Jesus Christ.

16

PERFECT PEYTON

Peyton's parents were high performers and highly respected. They wanted the same for their daughter, but she started suffering anxiety from the pressure of their expectations. It became especially hard when her parents, teachers, and coaches compared her with her successful older sister. The stress levels had gotten so great that she started cutting herself in the hope of finding some relief.

The Key of Realistic Expectations

This is going to be one of the most difficult chapters for you to read as parents of an anxious teen, because I'm going to challenge you to consider your own role in creating an anxious teen. We've looked at many factors that can contribute to anxiety, but we have to recognize that even though we are well motivated, our excessive expectations can inadvertently be a factor in our teen's anxiety.

We don't want to overpressure our teens, and we don't want to enable them to abdicate responsibility; it can be hard to find the right balance. Some teens, at least at some points in their lives, need to be pushed harder, and, as parents, we have an important role in that. However, when it comes to anxious teens, the more common problem is parents pushing our teens too hard for too long and in too many areas so that they become overwhelmed with pressure to succeed or with a fear of failure. I want to get to the falsehoods that are often at the root of the pressure we put on teens.

"YOU CAN DO IT ALL"

When I was a teen, I had only one pressure in my life, and that was to get good grades. But that pressure wasn't constant. We had exams twice a year, and only the exams in our last two years counted toward our final grades. Nowadays teens are being tested every week in multiple subjects, and they have to sustain that performance all year round for four years to maintain a minimum of a 4.0 GPA to qualify for certain colleges and scholarships.

I played soccer for our school, but there was no training or practice. We played once a week on a Saturday morning, and we didn't even know where we ranked in the league most of the time. We certainly didn't have anyone keeping stats on us. And athletic ability wasn't a factor on college applications.

On top of academics and athletics, our teens are expected to demonstrate to colleges that they volunteer in the community, lead in the church youth group, hold down various jobs, and so on.

But they simply cannot do it all—not without suffering serious consequences in their mental, emotional, and spiritual health. Many crash and burn when they do get to college.

"YOU MUST GET IN TO THE BEST COLLEGE"

A second falsehood is that not only must our kids get into college, but they must get into the *best* college. And given that the best colleges are usually the most expensive, they must also do well enough at school to get scholarships.

I say that this is a falsehood because many kids are just not gifted for college and would do much better pursuing a trade or starting a business. Many skilled tradesmen earn more than college graduates and have no debt to pay off. Also, it's simply not true that the best colleges guarantee the best outcomes. And even when kids do get an athletic scholarship, many kids experience burnout because they cannot keep both sports and academics going. Forty percent of those who go to college fail to finish.[1]

We do our kids a big favor when we honestly assess their abilities and gifting and help them pursue what best suits them rather than try to fit them into our mold or society's mold. Show them that you want to help them identify the unique way God has gifted them and that you want to help them develop these talents and express them in the service of God. They don't need to get into the best college to have a happy and successful life.

"YOU CAN DO ANYTHING IF YOU PUT YOUR MIND TO IT"

While kids will do a lot better at anything if they apply themselves more diligently, it is not true that they can do or be anything they want if only they will try harder. This belief ignores God's unique gifting of them, varying opportunities, and his providential plan. We must teach our kids to do whatever God has in mind for them and to pursue his will, not their own.

"FAILURE IS A DISASTER"

No one likes to fail. It's painful and often humbling. However, we will all fail at something eventually, and we must train our kids to fail well. We must create a context where it's okay to fail, where we see failure as a helpful guide to determine skills and talents. In many cases, our kids will actually perform better if we let them know that it's okay to fail as long as they do their best.

Perfection is impossible in this world, and it is a tyrannical master. So let's not impose that upon our kids. If we have to choose between a 4.0 GPA and a healthy teen, let's make sure we choose the latter.

Many teens, especially boys, are late developers and maturers. Sometimes they don't find their groove, their niche, until their early twenties. We need patience to wait for this and faith in God's

1. David McGrath, "Let's Quit Brainwashing Kids That It's a College Degree or Nothing," *Chicago Sun Times*, February 2, 2018, https://chicago.suntimes.com/columnists/lets-quit-brainwashing-kids-that-its-a-college-degree-or-nothing/.

care of them. Failure is not a disaster but can often be a blessing in disguise.

"ACHIEVEMENT IS MORE IMPORTANT THAN CHARACTER"

Kids who think their parents are more interested in achievement than their character usually have more troubles than other kids.[2] This is why the incidence of depression and anxiety is higher among the affluent than middle-class and poorer households. Often parents' expectations are far higher than their own level of achievement.

"PEOPLE WILL THINK LESS OF US"

And here we get to the crux of the issue. At times, our teens' performance is more to do with our reputation than with our kids' benefit. What will others think of us if our children fail to get into college? How good we will look if we have a perfect child in a perfect college in a perfect marriage, and so on.

Kids can detect when we are pursuing our own interest more than theirs and will ultimately resent it and eventually rebel against us. If we are grounding our identity in our kids' successes, then we are sacrificing them for us rather than us sacrificing for them.

Our relationship with our kids is far more important than what others think about us. Let's not create anxiety in them so that we can be proud in front of our peers. Whether people will think less of us or not (and most people hardly give us a second thought), it's far more important to ensure that our kids don't think less of us.

2. Richard Weissbourd, "The Overpressured Student," ASCD, May 2011, http://www.ascd.org/publications/educational-leadership/may11/vol68/num08/The-Overpressured-Student.aspx; Susanna Schrobsdorff, "Teen Depression and Anxiety: Why the Kids Are Not Alright," *Time*, October 27, 2016, http://time.com/4547322/american-teens-anxious-depressed-overwhelmed/.

TURNING THE KEY

1. *Comparison.* Just as social media tends to create a "compare and despair" mind-set, so we can inadvertently cause this in our kids. Ask yourself if you are contributing to this by comparing your depressed or anxious teen to:

- Yourself
- Another child in the family
- Your nieces and nephews
- Your friends' kids
- Your kid's classmates
- Your kid's teammates
- Cultural norms

2. *Uniqueness.* While we want to remove these negative forces from our relationships with our kids, on the positive side, we want to help them identify their unique God-given abilities and passions. We want to encourage them to develop these abilities, but without over-pressuring them. And above all, we want them to develop dependence upon God not upon themselves.

3. *Failure.* Help your children prepare for and learn from failure. Everybody fails at some point in their lives. The difference between people is how they respond to failure. Progress is more important than success and growth more important than perfection. Striving for progress is biblical (Col. 3:23), but striving for perfection is sinful.

4. *Cutting.* If your child is cutting herself or engaging in other kinds of self-harm (and boys do this too), understand that teens often do this to release emotional pain. Say something like, "I am so sorry that you are feeling so much pain. I am here to help you in any way I can." A professional counselor can help teens get to the roots of such actions as well as give them coping mechanisms and strategies to replace this with something healthy and positive. That may be exercise or something creative like painting. To encourage them that they can overcome this temptation, remind them of verses such as 1 Corinthians 10:13.

5. *Scale.* Show your kids that there is a scale or wide range between being a failure and being perfect in sports, grades, friends, feelings, and so on.

17

PARALYZED PAM

Decision-making paralyzed Pam. She was so scared of ruining her life and got so stressed about both big and small decisions that her health, her appetite, and her sleep were suffering. Full of self-doubt and questioning, she's started to question God's existence but is scared to ask for help.

The Key of Problem-Solving

It used to be so much easier, didn't it? You made all the decisions and you imposed them on your kids. Then the teen years come along, and we discover that our teens want to make decisions themselves, causing tension and anxiety for them and you. Is there any way to destress this part of life?

I've outlined a seven-step process for decision-making in *Why Am I Feeling Like This?* Help your teens learn this process and walk through it with them, even when the decisions seem easy. Perhaps you can help them watch you make decisions using the same process and let them listen in on your discussions as you think it through.

BE A CONSULTANT

Once they've learned the process and gone through a few examples under your supervision, you have to let them get on with it. But, initially, they have to come to you and seek your advice (that's step six). When they do, check that they've gone through the previous steps, and have them write out the way they worked through the process.

If they've done everything right, the best way to be a consultant is to start with questions. I've supplied questions in the teen book for the big decisions about calling, studies, and future work. But there are other questions for other areas like whom to marry, what car to buy, what clothes to wear, and so on. Here's a selection of general questions to choose from:

- Is this something that God's word clearly prohibits or commands?
- If not clearly forbidden or commanded, is there a general biblical principle that you can apply to this specific situation?
- What is your motive and aim in this?
- What have you already done to find out God's will and what do you plan to do?
- What options are you considering and what are the pros and cons of each?
- How much are you being influenced by other people's opinions?
- Who else have you consulted and what did they say?
- Which option will draw you closer to God and help you glorify God most?
- How will this decision impact your family, your church, your employer, others in your life? What other consequences can you foresee?
- How long have you been thinking and praying about this?
- How soon do you have to make a decision?
- Is there a command you can obey while you wait? Are you doing your duty today? Are you living in the light God has given you while you wait for him to give you more?
- What indicators of God's providence have you discerned?[1]

---

1. For these and other questions about guidance see Kevin DeYoung, *Just Do Something* (Chicago: Moody, 2009); James C. Petty, *Step by Step* (Phillipsburg, NJ: P&R, 1999); James Swavely, *Decisions, Decisions: How (and How Not) to Make Them* (Phillipsburg, NJ: P&R, 2003); and Sinclair Ferguson, *Discovering God's Will* (Edinburgh: Banner of Truth, 2013).

More specific questions may be required for more specific situations. For example, take the question "Whom shall I date/ marry?" The Bible does not tell any of us the specific answer to this. Instead, it provides sufficient general principles for the Christian to follow that can be framed as questions:

- As we must marry "only in the Lord" (1 Cor. 7:39; 2 Cor. 6:14), is this person a Christian?
- As patience and prayer are Christian virtues (Phil. 4:6; Isa. 40:31), are you exercising patience or rushing into something without prayer?
- As Scripture outlines the roles and responsibilities of a husband and wife (Eph. 5:22–33), is he/she willing to live according to this direction?

When we consider the matter of what we should wear, again we can find general biblical principles that can be turned into questions:

- Is this modest (Rom. 12:2; 1 Tim. 2:9; Titus 2:12; 1 Pet. 5:5)?
- Is it extravagant (Prov. 11:22; 1 Tim. 2:9; 1 Pet. 3:3–4)?
- Does this distinguish between the sexes (Gen. 1:27; Deut. 22:5; 1 Cor. 11:14–15)?
- How does this impact others (Matt. 18:6–7; Rom. 14:13; 1 Cor. 10:24; Phil. 2:4)?

SUPPORT IN FAILURE

Because we want to try and prevent costly failures in our children's lives, we will sometimes contradict their decisions when they are younger and impose our own. But as they get older and start earning their own money, they will want to start making their own decisions, and we have to be prepared for them to make mistakes and fail. Sometimes we can see it coming, but we have to step back and let them make mistakes that will ultimately be for their good.

For example, they may decide to buy a certain car with their own money. We might think their decision is foolish and is going to be costly to them, but we have to be willing to give our advice and then step back and let them make the mistake.

It's not easy to do, and even harder not to assume an "I told you so" attitude when it all goes belly-up! However, we are called to love them even in their failures and show them grace, help them to learn and recover, and encourage them as they rebuild for the future.

TALK ABOUT SPIRITUAL QUESTIONS

It's common for teens to pass through a time of questioning about the faith they have been brought up in, especially if they are like Pam and think carefully and deeply about things. We must not squelch these questions or react with fear or anger if they ask them. Instead, we want to encourage them to bring any doubts and questions to us and then carefully and thoughtfully help them navigate their way to reasoned-out faith. If you don't have answers, ask your pastor to help or to meet with your teen. Rather than encouraging doubt and unbelief, talking about tough questions and doubts should strengthen faith ultimately. Indeed, unless we take these questions seriously, we will create deeper spiritual problems in the long run.

TURNING THE KEY

This chapter focused on making decisions about bigger issues. What about making decisions about small everyday things?

1. *Distinguish between big and small questions.* We don't want our kids to have to go through the seven steps every time they get a text or think about what to wear. Some decisions and problems are minor and therefore should take limited time and thought.

2. *Clear up the big questions.* Oftentimes, if we can help our teens resolve the bigger and more important problems, the smaller decisions get much easier. They have the mental and emotional bandwidth and balance to think and decide without so much interference and background stress from unresolved bigger challenges.

3. *Remind teens that people forget.* What's big in our minds may be small in other people's minds. While our teens may be agonizing about how to reply to a text, the other person has probably already moved on. And even if they do make a misstep, people forget and move on. Therefore, they should make a decision, trust God with it, and then move on with life rather than ruminating and second-guessing.

18

LONELY LUKE

Being in a military family, Luke had moved around a lot, making it hard for him to make friends. His natural shyness made him tense and nervous in crowds. He usually kept himself to himself, which was easier to do at school than at church where everyone wanted to involve him. He's now refusing to go to church because he was embarrassed by a question he couldn't answer at youth group and everyone laughed.

The Key of Church

Given that there is so much healing in the Scriptures, in Christ, and in prayer, you would think that attending church, where all these are present in abundance, would be an easy and obvious solution for depressed and anxious teens.

Not so. Despite the number and volume of therapeutic resources available in the church, church is sometimes one of the hardest places for such teens to attend. You may have noticed your teen started making excuses to stop attending the youth group, then Sunday school, then the evening service, and maybe now hasn't gone to church for weeks or even months.

Perhaps you've already had shouting matches about it. Or, at least, you've concluded that your teen is not a believer or is in a really bad spiritual condition. That may or may not be so.

UNDERSTAND THE DIFFICULTY

It's hard for many adults to understand the experience of teen anxiety. Perhaps you could try to imagine the fear you would have if at two in the morning you heard a window being smashed downstairs, and someone going up the stairs to your kids' bedroom. At its worst that's what anxious teens are experiencing, especially when going into social settings like church.

They haven't made a decision to be fearful. It's an automatic response that is extremely difficult to control. Try to listen to their fears, to feel what they feel, in order to build sympathy and empathy. If they feel you understand, you will have a much greater hope of helping them to take steps back to church.

The first step, therefore, is to ask what they are afraid of and why. Try to get to details. Express understanding and sympathy not surprise or contempt. Instead of saying, "Oh, come on, that's nothing to be afraid of," say, "I can understand why that makes you afraid," or, "Lots of other kids are afraid of these things too."

TAKE SMALL STEPS

Shouting at your teens for not going to church, threatening them, manipulating them, and bribing them—none of these are going to work in the long term and often will make things worse, if anxiety is the root problem. If they are forced to go to church when they are not ready for it, then the fear of church will probably only get greater. It's better to take a gradual approach that exposes them slowly and progressively to what they are afraid of.

- *Step 1.* Start by staying home with them and watching a service together online via your church's livestream.
- *Step 2.* Go to a midweek service or some other occasion with smaller crowds. Or perhaps attend a church where you are not known for a few weeks to rebuild confidence.
- *Step 3.* When ready to return to a Sunday service in your own church, arrive late, leave early, and sit near the back to minimize social contact and social anxiety, and also to allow an unobtrusive way of escape if needed.

- *Step 4*. Start coming to church on time and staying a few minutes after. Perhaps arrange for a friend to speak briefly to your teen after the service.
- *Step 5*. As they get used to this, begin to move back toward normality. Perhaps, when you feel your teen is ready to mix with the young people again, ask a friend to protect him, shielding him from inappropriate questions or pressures and guiding him to a safe quiet place if stressors are taking a toll.

If done carefully, this graduated exposure should build confidence as each step is navigated successfully. If there's a hiccup along the way, go back to the previous step for a few more weeks. The same graduated exposure approach can be applied to other specific fears as well, ideally under the supervision of a skilled counselor. Perhaps you can start with images of what is feared or imagining scenarios. Praise your kids for every small step of progress made.

INFORM THE LEADERSHIP

You should explain to your pastor, and probably the youth group leader, about the challenges your teen is facing. Maybe give them *Why Am I Feeling Like This?* or this parent's guide to help them understand how best to shepherd anxious teens. Perhaps you could encourage the leaders to sing worship songs that include laments and expressions of fear to show how normal this is in the Christian life. There are many psalms that could help here. Ask them to be especially careful about saying things like "Anxiety is a sin," or "If you believed more, you wouldn't be afraid." Ask them to pray publicly for those who suffer with anxiety and depression. There's no need to pray for people by name, but even that general mention in prayer can be a huge encouragement to those with this affliction. It helps to normalize the abnormality.

EDUCATE THE MEMBERSHIP

As you probably know, there's a lot of ignorance about anxiety and other mental disorders in society and in the church. This could be a wonderful opportunity to begin a conversation about these matters and provide resources to equip the saints to minister better to people in the church and in their own families who have been suffering in silence for years.

The church could invite someone with knowledge to speak about these matters and suggest practical help. Again, there's no need to mention the name of the anxious teen, but simply to acknowledge that this is a common problem and we need help to learn about it and minister to sufferers in our midst.

Be careful to pick books and speakers who will take a holistic approach to anxiety and depression. We don't want to make things worse by using resources or speakers who will take an overly simplistic approach that makes anxiety and depression all and only about personal sin. But talking about these things in church will give others a voice and permission to speak of their own struggles.

CONTACT COUNSELORS

When a problem like this arises, we soon realize how much we need expert and experienced care. Yes, members and pastors can do a lot to help anxious teens. We can love them, understand them, encourage them, listen to them, speak truth to them, be patient with them, and so on. All that is wonderful and provides a wonderful basis for healing.

Sometimes, however, expertise is required, and that's where we often run into problems. How do we pick a counselor that will help and not undermine faith?

Pastors and elders have an important role here in making contact with professionals in the local community—doctors, psychologists, biblical counselors—to find those we can entrust with our precious teens. Ideally they will be Christians, but sometimes that is not necessary, as long as the person will not undermine a Christian worldview and will work with us. In most circumstances it is ideal if the counselor agrees to share with the parents or pastor what he or she is doing with the teen. Then we can be sure that we are working together and not against one another.

RECEIVE CARE FOR YOURSELF

Caring for a loved one with anxiety or depression takes a toll on us. We get stressed, worn out, and even burned out. Perhaps our own faith begins to waver and our hope is diminished. The church community is important for us too. We need our faith nourished and built up. We need to pray with God's people and hear God's voice. We need fellowship and support. Caregivers need care. We need to cast our cares upon the Lord knowing that he cares for us. But we also need others to share our burden. Look for someone sympathetic and confidential you can confide in.

TURNING THE KEY

In the teen's book I guide teens on how to start a fear project and a service project. You can help them with both.

1. *Identify.* Identify the fear or a service opportunity.

2. *Plan.* Write a plan to slowly and gradually face the fear and engage in the service. Remind them of Isaiah 43:2 and tell them that although it will be uncomfortable at first, they can do it and it will get easier. Avoidance only makes things worse and harder the next time.

3. *Encourage.* Record progress to encourage further progress. Thank God for every step taken to overcome fear or engage in service.

4. *Friends.* Encourage friends to send texts to your teen. Although Luke and others like him find it difficult to be around others, they feel very lonely, and texting is a good way to let them know they are not alone without causing them stress.

Conclusion
GROWING FREEDOM

This is a short book but there's a lot packed into it. So to conclude, let's step back from the details and take a look at the big picture. What are the general principles to bear in mind as you begin to work with your teen?

Understanding

You now have much more understanding of depression and anxiety than you had before you started this book. Although perhaps you are focused on all the work that needs to be done, getting an understanding of these disorders is half the battle. Knowledge and understanding is 50 percent of your task. If teens sense that you get it and get them, that itself will be tremendously healing for them and encourage them to work with you. This knowledge has also developed in you an instinct about what to say and do in various situations. Be confident that you now know a lot more than most people and that you are much better equipped for this challenge.

Hope

"Why is my son/daughter feeling like this?" "What can I do to help?" Maybe you started this book with these questions in mind. Well, now you don't only know the answer to the first question, but you also have a lot of answers to the second. If you felt helpless and didn't know what might help, you now have many practical ideas to start working on from each Turning the Key section. This itself should make you feel more hope and optimism. Yes, there are many things you can do to help your hurting teen.

Slow

There is a danger of trying too much or using too many keys to begin with. You don't want to overwhelm your teen—or yourself. It's far better to choose a couple of strategies that you think would give most return first, establish them as habits and practices, and then add another, then another. You will probably eventually settle on half a dozen or so solutions that will become a common part of their lives. Although you should see improvements in two to three weeks, you have to commit to six months of focused effort and then regular check-ins going forward.

Progress

Because it takes so long to see change, it's easy to get discouraged. That's why it's important to keep a journal of progress and record any improvements in any areas so that you can look back after each week or so and see how the Lord has helped you to make forward movement. Talk about these changes for the better to encourage further effort.

Partner

It's hard to do this on your own. Ideally, both parents should be involved in this recovery, although you may take different roles and focus on different areas. I also recommend involving your pastor if he has demonstrated interest in and support for people with mental health challenges. The same goes for a biblical counselor. I've mentioned a few times the advantage of consulting with a mental health professional.

Submit

It may be that progress is the best that's achieved. In other words, it's possible that our teens will carry a degree of anxiety or depression with them for a significant period of time and even the rest of their lives. This book cannot promise total healing for everyone. But it can promise progress if the right means are used. We need to submit to whatever level of restoration God gives and also accept that we and our teens may just have to live with an element of this in their lives. God ordains everything for good for his children who are teens and parents. Your teen's affliction is probably for your sanctification too.

Remember

It's possible that our teens will make a full recovery, but there's always the danger of falling back into the bad habits that were there before. If they have had an episode of anxiety or depression, they are vulnerable to another if they don't make the changes permanent. And if they do lapse, remember the lessons learned from the past and implement again. At least now you will know what works, and the recovery is usually quicker.

Encourage

A Christian with anxiety will often feel even more anxious or depressed because he or she thinks that Christians should never have these emotions. As we have seen, however, there are non-spiritual causes of anxiety. Indeed, some Christians with anxiety have more faith than those who temperamentally are more confident people. That's where God has an opportunity to show his strength in our weakness and that his grace is sufficient for us (2 Cor. 12:9). Also, people with anxiety and depression are often very sensitive to the feelings of others and can be wonderful comforters of suffering people.

Pray

Without God we can do nothing. Therefore, let's call upon his name for wisdom, courage, hope, and healing. Let's remember that he cares for us and our teens more than we do and is more than willing and able to help. Pray for your teen and with your teen. Pray that the Lord would rebuke the devil who always takes advantage of any mental or emotional disorder. Pray for the Holy Spirit of peace and joy in your teen's life.

This book has covered the basics, but if you want to read more or learn more, please visit whyamIfeelinglikethis.com, where you'll find videos and articles that will help you further on this journey to freedom.

GENERAL INDEX

SCRIPTURE INDEX

Also Available from David Murray

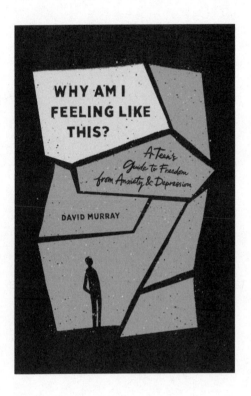

Counselor David Murray introduces readers to the personal stories of eighteen teens who have dealt with different types of anxiety or depression. From these accounts, Murray equips teens with keys to unlock the chains of anxiety and depression and experience new liberty, peace, and joy in their lives.

For more information, visit **crossway.org**.

Notes

Notes

Notes

Notes

Notes

Notes

Notes

Notes

Notes

Notes

Notes